LEARN TO
SUCCEED
AT
SELECTION
TESTS

LEARN TO
SUCCEED
AT
SELECTION
TESTS

GILLES AZZOPARDI

foulsham
LONDON • NEW YORK • TORONTO • SYDNEY

foulsham

The Publishing House, Bennetts Close, Cippenham,
Berkshire, SL1 5AP, England

ISBN 0-572-02619-6

This English language edition copyright © 2001
W. Foulsham & Co. Ltd

Originally published 1998 by Marabout, Belgium

Printed in Great Britain by The Bath Press, Bath.

CONTENTS

INTRODUCTION

You have decided to apply for a job: you've answered an advertisement or you have put yourself up for in-house promotion. This is only the beginning of a long and tortuous process during which you will be scrutinised, tested, observed from every angle, interviewed, short-listed and finally offered the job. Alternatively, your application may be consigned to the wastepaper bin.

How can you make sure that the odds are stacked in your favour? The two golden rules are, first, that you should abide by the rules and, second, that you leave no stone unturned in your quest for the ultimate goal – the job ! And to do this, you must be well acquainted with the methods that your prospective employers may use in order to make their final choice.

There are many different methods of selection and companies are using increasingly complex techniques to eliminate mistakes in their recruitment process as they search for their 'ideal candidate'; a great deal of time and money now goes into searching for the ideal selection procedure. One recent research study, carried out in France, questioned 837 head-hunters from 60 recruitment agencies and 42 internal corporate human resources departments to discover how the different selection methods were used and how effective they were. The study examined both frequency of use and reliability of different selection methods, including interviews, aptitude and intelligence tests, graphology samples, personality tests, role-playing and references. Interestingly, the two most popular methods – interviews (used by 99 per cent of selectors) and graphology (93 per cent) – proved not to be the most reliable. And the two most reliable, role-play and references, were actually found to be used by only 34 per cent and 28 per cent respectively.

External recruitment agencies favour personality tests. Some 61.5 per cent use them, as against 55 per cent of private companies and 69 per cent of larger companies. However, the latter are keener on aptitude tests: 84.5 per cent insist on applicants taking intelligence tests as opposed to 69 per cent of private companies and 55 per cent of agencies.

It is clear, then, that if you are to make the best of yourself in your search for success in selection, you must be prepared to undergo a large variety of tests. It is also true that the tests usually make the unprepared candidate nervous to some extent. The aim of this book is therefore not only to explain how the tests are applied but also to help you overcome any fears by familiarising you with the content and format of the tests. Better still, it will help you to boost your scores quite significantly.

This book will take you step-by-step through the most popular tests used by recruitment agencies and companies; the personnel they are targeted at (administrators, sales, IT executives, etc.); their frequency of use by recruiters and their aims and objectives. It also provides examples of the tests themselves, so that you can familiarise yourself with them (particularly useful for the administrative and intelligence tests); it evaluates your results; it tells you what traps to avoid; and, most importantly, it explains how to make yourself stand out from the crowd.

Playing the game

Can you refuse to answer a question on your private life or even refuse point-blank to take a test? In principle the answer is, yes, you can. Legally, a person applying for employment should be treated as an employee and has the same rights. You do not even have to respond to questions or take any tests that have no direct or essential link with the job on offer. Sexuality, religion, politics and union membership are beyond the remit of the interview process.

However, any refusal to co-operate is almost certain to lead to a failed application, so play the game. You may be shown a blurred ink blot, photo or drawing, which you are expected to interpret. You may even be asked to draw a tree or a house, to make colour associations – just do it.

Don't ask why or how. Don't try to be clever (so don't say, 'It's an ink blot') or too original; if they ask you to draw trees, just draw trees; if they want you to build houses, build 'normal' houses. Just go along with whatever they ask you to do, and answer the questions, however indiscreet, without trying to add humour or your personal opinion, or digressing from the matter in hand.

Show that you are willing, be inventive with the truth if you have to, but make sure you always play their game, their way.

TESTS FOR ADMINISTRATORS

Administrative tests, for example those where you are required to spot the mistake in a list of nouns or figures, are increasingly used by recruitment agencies and companies. This is a sector where many skills are required and selection is very demanding. Some recruiters simply ask candidates applying for an office or secretarial post to type a piece of text on the pretext that they are testing their typing speed. However, there may be one or two spelling or grammatical errors. So if you type the copy exactly as it is, without alteration, you may show that your English is not what it should be. On the other hand, if you correct the mistakes, you will prove that you are capable of thinking for yourself and taking the initiative.

You may be asked to take a test designed to evaluate your level of general knowledge and your basic skills (attention span, precision, speed of work, ability to concentrate for a given time, etc.).

TESTS FOR CLERICAL/ SECRETARIAL STAFF

The sample test given here is one of many tests used exclusively for administrative staff such as clerical workers, secretaries, etc., and is designed to evaluate the skills and performance of candidates in everyday office activities. It is not only the candidate's level of work that is under scrutiny but also their breadth of knowledge, the quality of their work, the speed with which it is carried out, and their general attention to detail.

The test examines eight major skills in the specific areas of maths, spelling, filing and secretarial skills. Whilst there is no time limit, the overall summing-up of the results does take into account the time taken as well as the number of correct answers.

These are a few examples of the sorts of questions you might be asked.

Maths
A number of different mathematical processes are tested.

For example:

1. $3.24 \times 16 \times 0.11 =$

2. $3912 \div 0.33 =$

3. $46 + (327 - 26) =$

4. $4312 - (28 \times 5) =$

5. $18 \text{ cm} + 7 \text{ mm} - 3.65 \text{ cm} =$

Spelling
A number of elementary spelling mistakes are presented in a text that you are given to correct. For example:

Correct the mistakes in the following paragraph:

Dinner had already started when I went down to the dining room and Frank was sitting at the table with his asociates, all talking and gesticulating in such an animated fashion it seemed that no-one was listening to what anyone else was saying. Aparently, they were discussing the relitive merits of the chef at this hotel and those of a certain Michel, a chef from a small Worcershire hotel that they had visited on a conferance weekend many years before. It was such a long time ago, he would definitely be retired by now – if indeed he was still alive – so the whole dispute was hyperthetical in any event. I stood looking at the table and watching this group of close coleagues for some moments before Frank noticed me out of the corner of his eye.

'Charles, he cried, getting up from his chair to come and greet me with a warm handshake. 'I had almost given you up for lost. These are my friend's – do come and meet them'

Write in the plural:

The black box has been mislaid.

Put the following sentence into the past tense:

Saturday is an exciting day because on this particular Saturday during May, we are going out after dinner to see a play.

Change this direct speech into indirect speech:

'I want those letters finished by the end of the day,' he told me, 'and make sure you check everything carefully.'

Attention to detail
This exercise consists of comparing two lists of names and telephone numbers and spotting the mistakes. For example:

Put a cross by any line in which you find a mistake:

Mrs Houseman 0208 765 8760	Mrs Houseman 0208 765 8760
John Metcalfe 01747 876296	John Metcalfe 01747 8761296
Mrs Simonds 0118 764 9870	Mrs Simmonds 0118 764 9870
Doctor Goddard 01584 129648	Doctor Godard 01584 129648
P Marchmont 0207 830 5729	P Marchmont 0207 820 5729
Olaa Mohammed 016 872 9740	Olaa Muhammed 018 872 9740
Ms Sarah Hardcastle 475927	Ms Sarah Hardcastle 475927
Mr Wontner-Smith 870356	Mr Wontner Smith 870356

Alphabetical classification
Add these names in alphabetical order to the list that follows:

(You will be given about 20 names to be added to a list of over 70.)

Classification according to several criteria
This sort of task would involve a card index that requires filing in alphabetical order according to three different criteria, such as company names, type of business, address.

Insurance classification
You may be given a list of insurance policies from which you have to select those which fulfil three given criteria, such as type of contract, nature of guarantees, the date the policy was taken out, etc.

Writing a synopsis

You will be given a text of about 20 lines to read before selecting the three main ideas outlined in the text from a given list. For example:

> 'In 1999 Macao is expected to revert to Chinese rule after being a Portuguese colony, and China has high hopes that in the process they may convince Taiwan, the final frontier, to accept reunification on the same basis of 'one country, two systems' as was promised to the residents of Hong Kong. As for Singapore, outside the geographical boundaries of the Empire, it would finally become 'unmasked' as the Chinese colony of South East Asia, which encompasses Indonesia, Vietnam, Malaysia and Thailand. China would thus be in full possession once again of its errant children, those who are known as the overseas Chinese, the four island-emirates of the China Sea, which are already, in terms of investment in Asia, devouring the ferocious Chinese dragon.'

Tick the three most important ideas in the text in the following list:

1. Macao will become Chinese in 1999.

2. Taiwan is the final frontier.

3. The Chinese reunification is based on the 'one country, two systems' principle.

4. Singapore is the 'Chinese colony' of South East Asia.

5. Singapore is not within the geographical boundaries of the Chinese empire.

6. The four island-emirates of the China Sea are the overseas Chinese.

7. Hong Kong, Macao, Taiwan and Singapore invest more in Asia than Japan does.

Writing a summary

This exercise consists in reorganising a piece of given text·into a logical order: for example, putting into chronological order the biography of a famous author, made up of 14 sentences that are jumbled up.

SOLUTIONS

Maths

1. $3.24 \times 16 \times 0.11 = 5.7024$

2. $3912 \div 0.33 = 11854.54$

3. $46 + (327 - 26) = 347$

4. $4312 - (28 \times 5) = 4172$

5. $18 \text{ cm} + 7 \text{ mm} - 3.65 \text{ cm} = 15.05 \text{ cm}$

Spelling

There are eight spelling mistakes in the paragraph: associates; apparently; relative; Worcestershire; conference; hypothetical; colleagues; friends.

There should also be a quotation mark after Charles and a full stop before the quotation mark at the end of the final sentence.

In the plural

The black boxes have been mislaid.

In the past tense

Saturday was an exciting day because on that particular Saturday during May, we were going out after dinner to see a play.

In indirect speech

He told me that he wanted the letters finished by the end of the day and that I was to be sure to check everything carefully.

Attention to detail

You should have put a cross against the following:

Line 2: an additional 1 in the telephone number.

Line 3: an additional m in the name.

Line 4: a d has been omitted.

Line 5: 830 has become 820.

Line 6: o has become u and 6 has become 8.

Line 8: the hyphen is missing.

Writing a synopsis
1, 3 and 7 should be ticked.

NUMBER AND LETTER TESTS

There are several different styles of intelligence test, and they are very widely used: nowadays, 63 per cent of large companies and recruitment agencies include them in their selection procedures. All the tests are based on the same logical premises and are often less complicated than they appear. With a bit of practice you can achieve excellent results.

Tests involving logical series of numbers and letters are designed to evaluate the candidate's ability to think on their feet and to solve problems of all different types quickly. They are used by about 14 per cent of agencies and companies. The ones reproduced in this chapter are known as the R 80 and the R 85.

FORMAT

Each test has two stages. The examiner gives you time to familiarise yourself with the type of exercises used. Then you will be asked to solve 40 problems in 20 minutes (using a stopwatch). The number of right and wrong answers you get will each be added up.

During the test the examiner will be looking at how you work: whether you scribble or write neatly; whether you answer quickly, dry up on a difficult question, etc. The tester will be taking into account both the score and the way you work.

EXAMPLES

Answer all the questions on the following pages

> EITHER by replacing the dashes with numbers, letters or an appropriate word (a letter or a number must be inserted for each dash)

> OR by underlining the correct letters, numbers or words to continue the sequence, make a matching pair, etc.

You have 20 minutes to solve the 40 questions below.

1. 7 1 3 4 2 6 3 8 7 4 7 9 5 1

2. piano, violin, saxophone, guitar, double bass

3. a ̲ i o u

4. 666 (S) 421 (F) 955 (N) 147 (−)

5. 1 5 9 13 −

6. A D G J −

7. AE BF CG DH − −

8. J 2 G 5 D 8 − −

9. sweet, savoury; dry, wet ; soft, − − − −

10. leap, flea; pale, − − − −

11. 5 2 4 1 3 −

12. 3 6 5 10 9 −

13. AZ BC YX DEF − − −

14. Rediscover, discover, cover, − − − −

15. tiger I   wild II   animal III
    stone 3   diamond 1   − − − − − − −2

16. 3 6 5 15 14 − − − −

17. A1 BC2 DEF6 GHIJ−

18. II2   VI3   V2   XV4
    XX4   VII4 III3   XIV−

19. | high | soft | cold | low | hot |
    | heavy | night | light | white | day |

20. | I2 | A1 | R3 | AIR | | |
    | M4 | L2 | F1 | E5 | A3 | – – – – – |

21. 0   2   6   12   – –

22. A   C   E   G   I   –   –

23. 1A   2D   3I   4P   – –

24. 5 3 <u>1</u> 6 7 3 <u>4</u> 6 8 <u>9</u> 5 7 1 2 5 16 3 7

25. apricot, cherry, peach, <u>orange</u>, avocado, shark, dolphin, swordfish, perch, skate

26. wool, hemp, cotton, <u>silk</u>, linen

27. 3   9   27   81   – – –   – – –

28. DBAC   HFEG   LJIK   PNM–

29. | nightfall | dawn | morning | daybreak |
    | 9 | 4 | 7 | – |

30. 7   13   8   12   –   11   – –

31. A   D   I   P   –

32. white, black; before, after; short, – – – –

33. time, rats; emit, – – – –

34. 12B   23F   34L   45–

35. untransportable, transportable, portable, – – – – –

36. C G L R –

37. <u>Moon</u>, Mercury, Venus, Mars, Jupiter
    Rome, New York, Paris, Madrid, Brussels

38. 211   911   1   11;   T   N   O   –

39. <u>cube</u>, square, circle, cone, triangle

40. | N3 | I2 | G1 | A4 | GINA; | | |
    | W1 | A6 | I5 | M7 | L4 | I2 | L3 | – – – – – – – |

SOLUTIONS

1. 7 1 3 4 2 6 3 8 7 4 7 9 5 1
   1, 2, 3, 4, 5, is a sequence.

2. piano, violin, saxophone, guitar, double bass
   The piano and the saxophone are the odd ones out as they
   are not string instruments.

3. a e i o u
   The vowels in alphabetical order.

4. 666 (S) 421 (F) 955 (N) 147 (O)
   The letters are the initials of the numbers: Six hundred and
   sixty six, Four hundred and twenty one, etc.

5. 1 5 9 13 17
   Each number is obtained by adding 4 to the previous one.

6. A D G J M
   Each letter is separated from the following one by the two
   intervening letters: A (bc) D (ef) G (hi) J (kl) M.

7. AE BF CG DH EI
   Each letter in the pair makes up two separate alphabetical
   sequences: A, B, C, D, E and E, F, G, H, I.

8. J 2 G 5 D 8 A 11
   Each letter is separated from the following one by two other
   letters (in reverse alphabetical order). Each number is
   obtained by adding 3 to the previous one.

9. sweet, savoury; dry, wet; soft, hard
   Pairs of opposites.

10. Leaf.

These are simple anagrams.

11. 5 2 4 3 1 0
    The sequence progresses in increments of −3, +2:
    5 (−3) = 2 (+2) = 4 (−3) = 1 (+2) = 3 (−3) = 0

12. 3 6 5 10 9 18
    The sequence progresses in increments of ×2, −1:
    3 (×2) =6 (−1) = 5 (×2) = 10 (−1) = 9 (×2) = 18

13. A Z BC YX DEF <u>WVU</u>
There are two alphabetical sequences, one moving in the usual order, A, BC, DEF; the other in reverse order, Z, YX, WVU, with an extra letter being added each time.

14. rediscover, discover, cover, <u>over</u>
A sequence, where letters are removed from the start of each word to form another word.

15. tiger I   wild II   animal III
stone 3   diamond 1   <u>precious 2</u>
The diamond is a precious stone as the tiger is a wild animal. The numbers indicate word order, in the first case in Roman numerals and in the second in Arabic numbers.

16. 3 6 5 15 14 <u>56</u> <u>55</u>
The sequence is formed by multiplying the first number by 2, then subtracting 1; then multiply this number by 3 and then subtract 1; then multiply this number by 4 and subtract 1 as follows:
$3 \times 2 = 6 - 1 = 5 \times 3 = 15 - 1 = 14 \times 4 = 56 - 1 = 55$

17. A1   BC2   DEF6   GHIJ<u>24</u>
The numbers increase each time by multiplying the previous one by the number of letters which follow it.

18. II2   VI3   V2   XV4   XX4   VII4   III3   XIV<u>5</u>
Each Arabic number is equal to the number of lines that make up the Roman numerals.

19. high   <u>soft</u>   cold   low   hot
heavy   night   light   <u>white</u>   day
'White' is the only one in the second group that has no opposite, in the same way that 'soft' has no opposite in the first group.

20. I2   A1   R3   AIR
M4   L2   F1   E5   A3   <u>FLAME</u>
The number following each letter shows its position in the complete word.

21. 0 2 6 12 <u>20</u>
    The sequence is 1, 2, 3, 4, 5, obtained by calculating the
    square of each number then subtracting the original number
    from the result:
    $1^2 - 1 = 0$, $2^2 - 2 = 2$, $3^2 - 3 = 6$, $4^2 - 4 = 12$, $5^2 - 5 = 20$

22. A C E G I <u>K M</u>
    The sequence shows alternate letters in the alphabet:
    A(b)C(d)E(f)G(h)I(j)K(l)M.

23. 1A 2D 3I 4P <u>5Y</u>
    Each number squared indicates the place of the letter in the
    alphabet: so 5 squared equals Y, the 25th letter.

24. 5 3 1 6 7 3 4 6 8 9 5 7 1 2 5 16 3 7
    A sequence of numbers (1,2,3,4) squared.

25. apricot, cherry, peach, <u>orange</u>, avocado
    shark, <u>dolphin</u>, swordfish, perch, skate
    Dolphin is the only mammal in the group as 'orange' is the
    only fruit in the group without a kernel.

26. <u>wool</u>, hemp, cotton, <u>silk</u>, linen
    Both are animal fibres.

27. 3 9 27 81 <u>243</u> <u>729</u>
    Each number in the sequence is obtained by multiplying the
    previous one by 3.

28. DBAC HFEG LJIK   <u>PNMO</u>
    In each group of letters the last one precedes the first one in
    alphabetical order.

29. nightfall dawn morning daybreak   9 4 7 <u>8</u>
    The numbers indicate the number of letters in each word.

30. 7 13 8 12 <u>9</u> 11 <u>10</u>
    The sequence is obtained by alternately adding and
    subtracting by a number which is reduced by one each time:
    7 (+ 6) = 13 (- 5) = 8 (+ 4) = 12 (- 3) = 9 (+ 2) =
    11 (- 1) = 10

31. A D I P <u>Y</u>
    The position of the letter in the alphabet corresponds to the sequence of the square of numbers 1, 2, 3, 4, 5, from A, (1^2) to Y, (25^2).

32. white, black; before, after; short, <u>long</u>
    Pairs of antonyms.

33. time, rats; emit, star
    Reverse the order of the letters of each word in the first pair to give the words in the second pair.

34. 12B   23F   34L   45<u>T</u>
    The product of the numbers gives the position of the letter in the alphabet:
    $4 \times 5 = 20 = T$, the 20th letter.

35. untransportable, transportable, portable, <u>table</u>
    Shed letters from the beginning of each word to form a new word each time.

36. C   G   L   <u>R</u>
    The number of letters between the given letters increases by one each time.
    (ab)C(def)G(hijk)L(mnopq)R.

37. <u>Moon</u>, Mercury, Venus, Mars, Jupiter
    Rome, <u>New York</u>, Paris, Madrid, Brussels
    New York is not a capital, just as the Moon is not a planet.

38. 211   911   1   11;   T   N   O   <u>E</u>
    The letters are the initials of the preceding numbers if written out in script.

39. <u>cube</u>, square, circle, <u>cone</u>, triangle
    The two underlined are solid shapes; the others are two-dimensional.

THE DOMINO TEST

Tests devised to evaluate your powers of logic are designed also to show your general level of intelligence. One of the most common, the Domino Test, is used by the British Army to recruit cadets. Again, there are several different types of domino test. In this chapter there are two examples, Anstay's D 48 and D 70, which are typical of those most frequently used in selection procedures.

FORMAT

Each test shows 40 domino patterns to be completed. Four examples are given with explanations at the start. The test lasts exactly 25 minutes. Ten minutes before the end the examiner will give you a time warning.

The problems become increasingly difficult as the test progresses and only 3.6 per cent of all candidates obtain the maximum score. By practising, however, you can improve your score considerably. Each problem scores 1 point, regardless of the level of difficulty. The average time available per problem is only 37.5 seconds, so you should move rapidly on to the next problem if you get stuck.

EXAMPLES

Each drawing represents a group of dominoes. The number of dots on each half of the domino can vary from 0 to 6. Look at each group and find the value of the missing domino. Write the corresponding numbers for this domino on the answer sheet.

Group 1

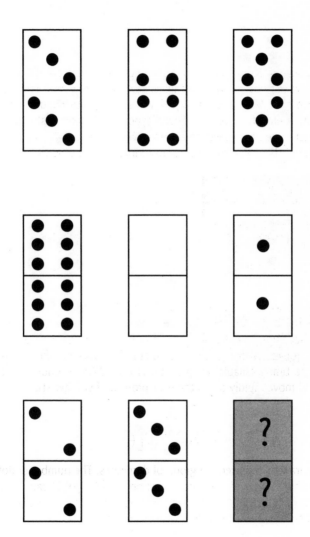

Group 2

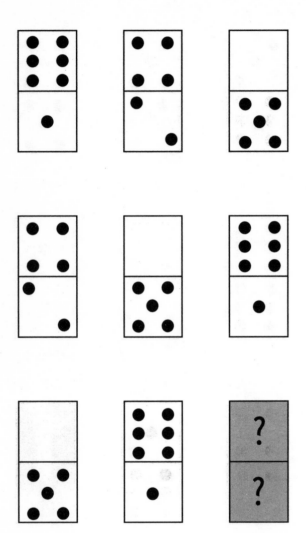

Group 3

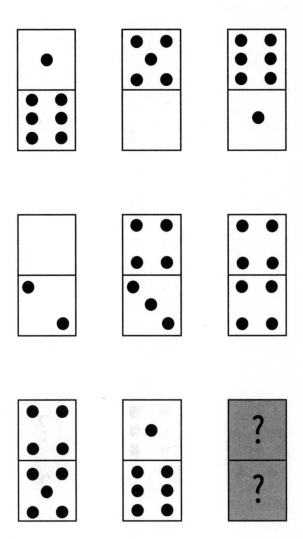

Group 4

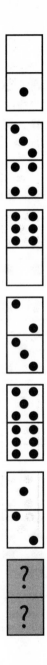

Group 5

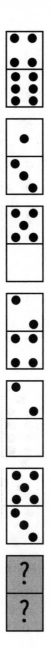

Group 6

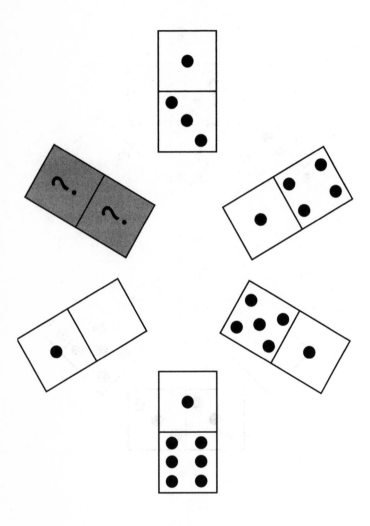

Group 7

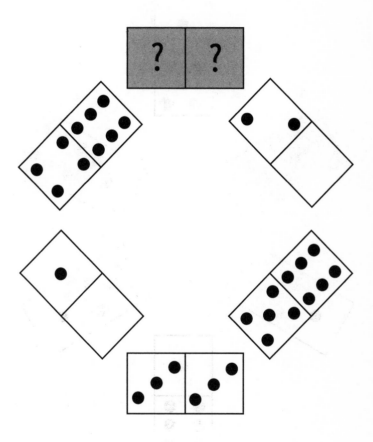

Group 8

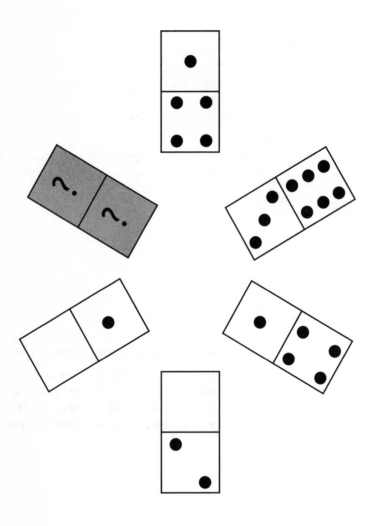

SOLUTIONS

Group 1: Each line presents a sequence of 'doubles':
(3, 4, 5), (6, 0, 1), (2, 3, 4)

Group 2: The same three dominoes appear on each line in a different order.

Group 3: On each line the top value of the right hand domino equals the sum of the two preceding values:
(1 + 5 = 6), (0 + 4 = 4), (4 + 1 = 5)
The lower squares make a sequence:
6, 0, 1, 2, 3, 4, 5, 6, 0

Group 4: Each domino 'jumps' a value:
0/1, (2), 3/4, (5), 6/0, (1), 2/3, (4), 5/6, (0), 1/2, (3), (4/5)

Group 5: Using the central domino (2/4) as a starting point, two sequences are established in which a value is missed out between each two halves of each domino:
moving upwards: 2, (1), 0, (6), 5, (4), 3, (2), 1, (0), 6, (5), 4
moving downwards: 4, (3), 2, (1), 0, (6), 5, (4), 3, (2), (1), (0), (6)

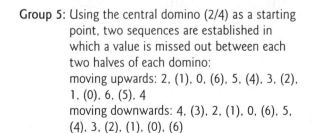

Group 6: The value 1 alternates between the outside and the inside. Starting from 3, the values go upwards in sequence, alternating between inside and outside: 3, 4, 5, 6, 0, 1

Group 7: Taking 6/4 as a starting point and going anti-clockwise, we have:
a diminishing sequence where the values of each half jump one:
6, (0), 1, (2), 3, (4), 5, (6), 0, (1), 2
and an increasing sequence where the values of each half jump two:
4, (5, 6), 0, (1, 2), 3, (4, 5), 6, (0, 1), 2, (3, 4), 5

Group 8: On the outside the values progress from one to the next by omitting the intervening value each time:
1, (0), 6, (5), 4, (3), 2, (1), 0, (6), 5
On the inside the sum of the values directly opposed in the circle is always equal to 4:
$4 + 0 = 3 + 1 = 1 + 3$

THE PLAYING CARD TEST

Playing cards may also be used in intelligence tests. The test given here is Pire's MGM test, designed in 1957, which is often considered to be an adaptation of the Domino Test (see page 24), using different materials. The aims of both are very similar: to evaluate powers of logic and the ability of the candidate to construct rational groupings not necessarily based on their contents. The rules are identical to the Domino Test. The only difference lies in the use of zero values (jokers), and in the greater variety of the cards and number of unknowns available.

Many experts in the field consider the material too 'colourful' for any objective measurement of logic and so prefer the Domino Test.

FORMAT

The test consists of a series of 40 different configurations of cards which you have to complete. You have 25 minutes in which to do so, which is a little over 37 seconds per problem. Each problem you solve scores 1 point, regardless of how difficult it is.

EXAMPLES

The examiner will explain that the hidden cards are dependent on the organisation of the other cards and that any jokers are to be ignored.

For practice, try to solve the eight problems that follow in 5 minutes.

Group 1

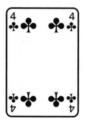

Group 2

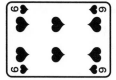 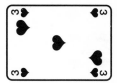

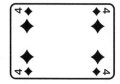 

Group 3

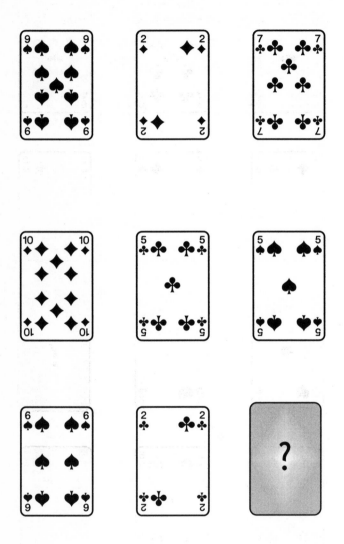

Group 4

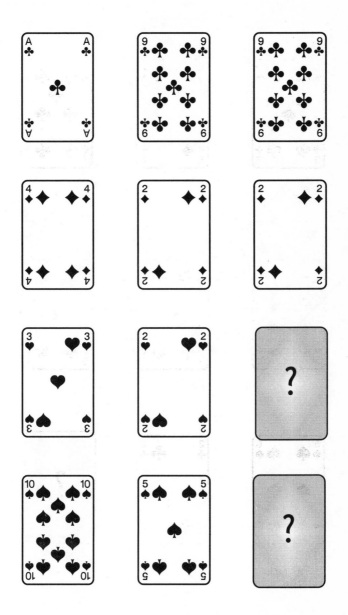

Group 5

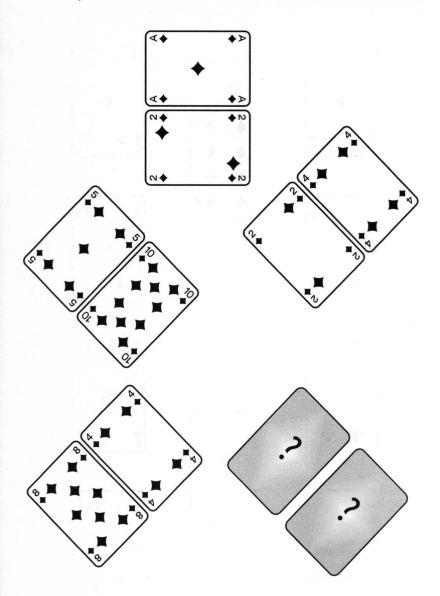

Group 6

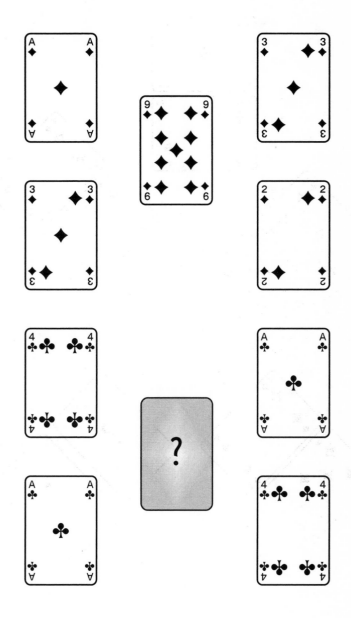

Group 7

Group 8

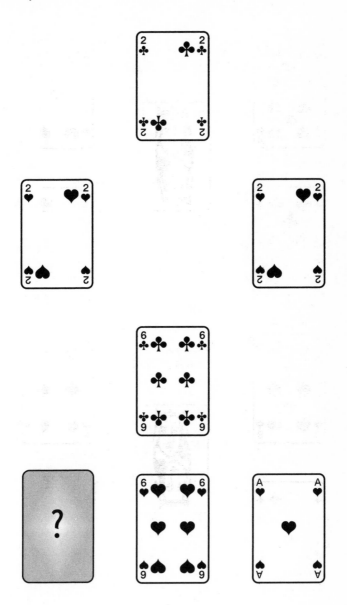

SOLUTIONS

Group 1: A run of the four suits (spades, diamonds, clubs, <u>hearts</u>), decreasing in value by 3 each time:
10 (spades) − 3 = 7 (diamonds) − 3
= 4 (clubs) − 3 = 1 (Ace of hearts)

Group 2: The cards are lined up in pairs of the same suit (hearts, <u>clubs</u> and diamonds), the sum of each of which is 9.

Group 3: Each horizontal sequence shows the three same suits in a different order (hearts, <u>diamonds</u>, clubs). The value of the card on the right is equal to the difference of the values of the two preceding cards: 9 − 2 = 7, 10 − 5 = 5, 6 − 2 = <u>4</u>

Group 4: Each horizontal sequence contains only one suit. On the first and third lines the value of the left-hand card is equal to the product of the two preceding values:
1 × 9 = 9, 3 × 2 = <u>6</u>
On the second and the fourth lines it is equal to the quotient of the values:
4 ÷ 2 = 2, 10 ÷ 5 = <u>2</u>

Group 5: A single suit: <u>diamonds</u>.
Going in a clockwise direction from the
ace of diamonds and alternating from
the outside to the inside of each pair, the
sequence of values is 1, 2, <u>3</u>, 4, 5.
By alternating from the two of
diamonds (in the top centre inside
position), the sequence of values is
2, 4, <u>6</u>, 8, 10.

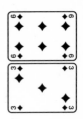

Group 6: There are two groups of five cards, one group
being diamonds and the other clubs. The
value of the central card is equal to the sum
of the value of each of the suit groupings:
1 + 3 + 3 + 2 = 9 (diamonds)
and 4 + 1 + 4 + 1 = <u>10</u> (<u>clubs</u>)

Group 7: Each horizontal pair of cards are of the same
suit, and on each line the difference between
the values is equal:
10 − 5 = 7 − 2 = 5
and 8 − 6 = 3 − 1 = <u>2</u>

Group 8: Reading the lines of cards horizontally, the
suits are identical:
clubs, hearts, clubs, <u>hearts</u>
Reading vertically, the total value of the cards
in each line increases by 2:
2, 4 (2+2), 6, 8 (<u>1</u>+6+1)

DIAGRAMS (1) RAVEN'S MATRIX 47

Sequences of diagrams are commonly used in intelligence tests. The first problems we shall look at in this section are examples of Raven's Matrix 47, a system of testing frequently used in the recruitment of scientific personnel (engineers, IT specialists, etc.). You may also come across the PM 38, a simplified version generally used for students with A-levels. With both it is best to finish as many problems as possible and then return to any troublesome ones if time allows, rather than waste valuable time agonising over them.

AIM

To measure the candidate's levels of perception, observation and reasoning.

FORMAT

The test consists of 48 series of diagrams which have to be completed by selecting one of the given options. Duration of the test is 40 minutes. Halfway through, the examiner will tell you how much time remains. Once again the problems become increasingly difficult. The average time allowed for each problem is 50 seconds. Each correct response scores 1 point.

EXAMPLES

Give yourself 5 minutes to solve the six problems that follow. Complete each diagram by selecting one of the numbered options.

Test 1

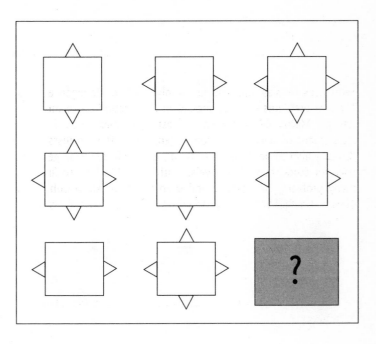

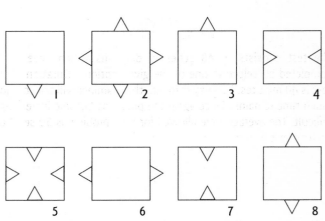

Test 2

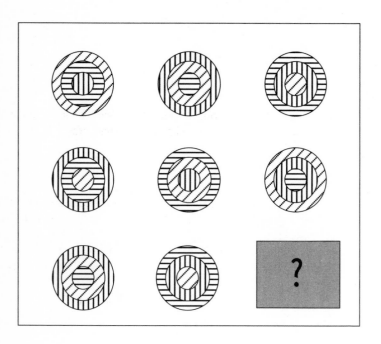

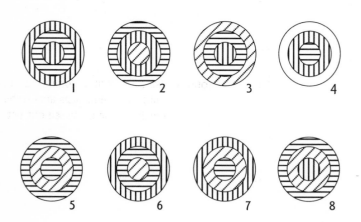

Test 3

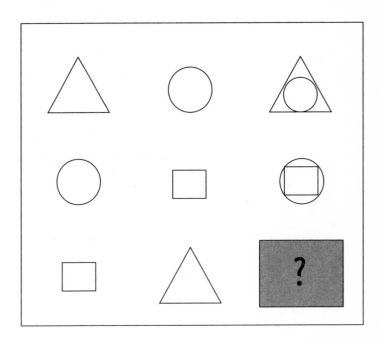

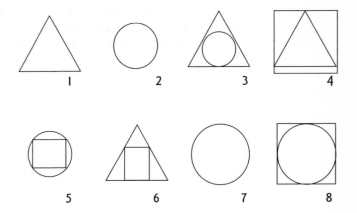

Test 4

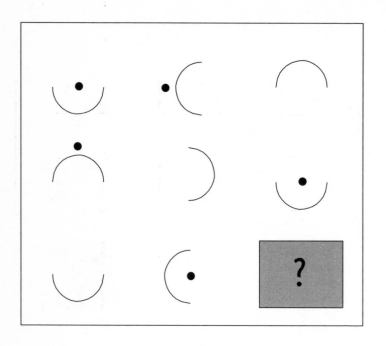

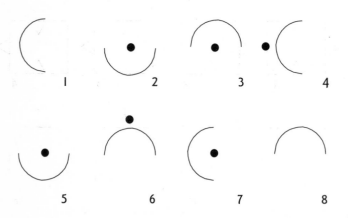

Test 5

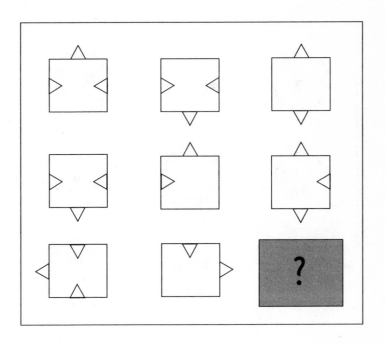

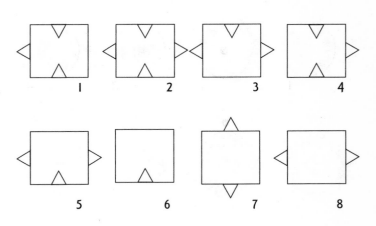

Test 6

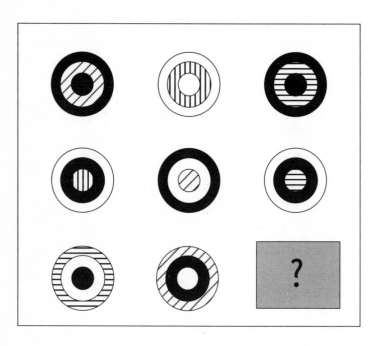

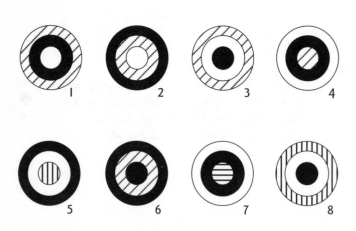

SOLUTIONS

Test 1: Diagram 8
The same three diagrams appear on each
horizontal line in a different order.

Test 2: Diagram 3
Each diagram contains three motifs: vertical,
horizontal and diagonal stripes. These occur in
a different order on each line.

Test 3: Diagram 6
On each horizontal line, the right-hand
drawing is obtained by superimposing the two
preceding diagrams.

Test 4: Diagram 6
On each line the arc turns clockwise by 90
degrees. In each set of three diagrams, the dot
appears once on the inside and once on the
outside, and once completely disappears.

Test 5: Diagram 5
By superimposing the first two diagrams on
each horizontal line, you create the right-
hand diagram. When the small triangles on
the inside are superimposed they are
obliterated.

Test 6: Diagram 8
There is one vertically striped, one horizontally
striped and one diagonally striped ring on each
horizontal line of diagrams. The plain rings
alternate between being black and white.

DIAGRAMS (2) BONNARDEL'S BV 53

Like the Matrix 47 problems in the previous chapter, this style of test, known as Bonnardel's BV 53, is often used for the recruitment of scientific personnel. It is based on the same principles of logic, although the diagrams are different.

EXAMPLES

Give yourself 5 minutes to solve the six problems below.

Test 1

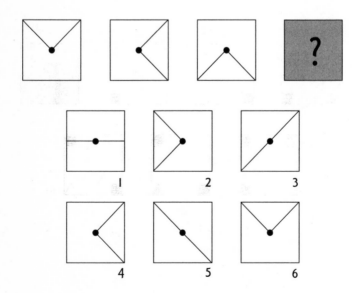

Test 2

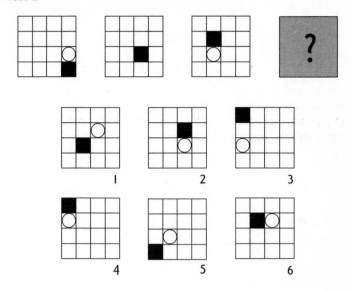

Test 3

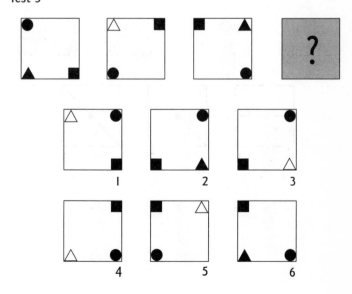

Test 4

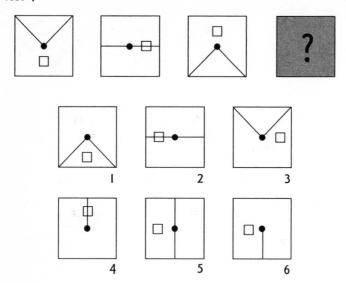

Test 5

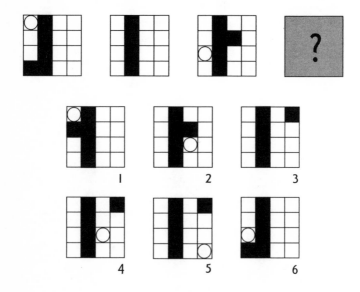

Test 6

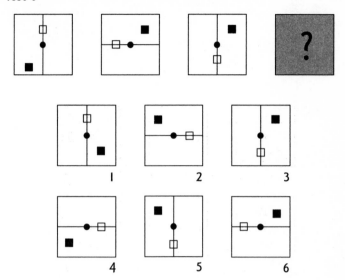

SOLUTIONS

Test 1: Diagram 2
The lines on the inside of the square turn clockwise through 90 degrees each time.

Test 2: Diagram 3
The circle moves horizontally from right to left, one square at a time; the square moves diagonally upwards, also one square at a time.

Test 3: Diagram 3
The circle and the square move anti-clockwise to the next corner, whilst the triangle moves the same distance in the opposite direction (i.e. clockwise), changing colour with each move.

Test 4: Diagram 6
The right-hand line moves 45 degrees clockwise each time with the left-hand line moving by the same amount anti-clockwise. The small white square moves round 90 degrees anti-clockwise.

Test 5: Diagram 3
The circle zigzags from top to bottom, one square at a time. The square moves diagonally upwards. Both disappear into the black column, which remains constant.

Test 6: Diagram 4
The line bearing the small white square moves anti-clockwise by 90 degrees, whilst the small black square moves with the line in the same direction but crosses the line each time.

TESTS FOR IT PERSONNEL

The tests in this chapter are increasingly used in companies specifically recruiting personnel with information technology skills, both beginners and experienced staff.

AIM

To obtain an overall picture of the way in which your mind is organised.

FORMAT

There are five different tests, each designed to test ability in a specific area:

A verbal comprehension test (8 minutes long) to test your ability to express yourself in non-technical language.

A reasoning test (20 minutes long) to evaluate your ability to translate problems expressed in mathematical symbols.

A logic test (18 minutes long) designed to test your ability to decode symbols.

A numerical aptitude test (6 minutes long) to evaluate your mental arithmetic skills.

A diagram test (25 minutes long) to test your analysis and problem-solving skills.

DURATION OF TEST

1 hour 17 minutes in total.

EXAMPLE

This test is designed to test your skill in reasoning and in formulating problems in a straightforward way by using common mathematical symbols. Read the problem and select the correct solution.

A shop offers a reduction of r% on an item which was originally priced up at P pence. The new price for the item is:

 A. $P - r$ pence

 B. $r \times P/100$ pence

 C. $P - (r \times P \div 100)$ pence

 D. $P - (r/100)$ pence

 E. $P \div (r \times 100)$ pence

IMPORTANT NOTES

The problems, particularly in the logic and diagram sections, are sometimes of a highly complex and unfamiliar nature. A good preparation for the tests would be to practice the problems found in Chapters 2 and 3.

Solution to the example
C

PERSONALITY TESTS (1) – THE GUILFORD–ZIMMERMAN TEST

Over 60 per cent of large companies and recruitment agencies use personality questionnaires in their selection procedures. Although there are some differences, the tests usually consist of statements or representations of situations, followed by a choice of responses. The candidates select the response they consider to be most appropriate or closest to their own reaction.

The Guilford-Zimmerman (GZ) Test is the best known and most widely used of all the personality tests. It aims to define ten personality traits: general level of activity, sociability, emotional stability, objectivity, influence over others, ability to think things through, kindness towards others, personal relationships, masculinity and resistance to constraints.

FORMAT

The test has 300 statements, each with three possible responses: Yes, No or Don't know, shown as ?.

EXAMPLE

Read each sentence carefully. If the statement applies to you, circle the answer 'Yes'. If this statement does not apply to you, circle 'No'. If you don't know or cannot make up your mind, then circle '?'; however, try to avoid the latter wherever possible.

A. I like speaking in public.   Yes – No – ?

B. I have a lot of friends.   Yes – No – ?

C. I enjoy reading books on philosophy.   Yes – No – ?

DURATION OF TEST

Variable, about 50 minutes.

POINTS TO WATCH

It may be tempting to respond with a Don't know (?) but this should be avoided if you don't wish to be categorised as someone who can be inconsistent.

HOW YOU SCORE

Each answer is worth one point on the credit or debit tally for that particular personality trait. For example, by circling 'Yes' for statement A, you increase your 'Influence' score. However, if you circle 'No', you are decreasing it. In the same way, a 'Yes' to statement B adds one point to your sociability credit rating and 'No' to statement C takes away one point from your 'ability to think things through' rating.

PERSONALITY TESTS (2) — CATTELL'S 16 PF

Used by 26 per cent of agencies and companies, this test is very similar to the GZ test (see page 61) in both presentation and aims. It aims analyse your reactions to situations and those areas of your life that are of most interest to you. The questions are simple and there are no catches. You should reply quickly and sincerely. There is no such thing as a correct or incorrect answer: each of us is an individual and there is a huge range of personality types.

AIM

To establish a personality profile from the levels of these 16 personality traits: introversion, extroversion, intelligence, emotional stability, self-confidence, conscientiousness, timidity, impulsiveness, practicality, toughness, willingness to trust others, straightforwardness, anxiety, independence, self-control and moderation. The combination of all these criteria enable the personality to be categorised in relation to four major axes: anxiety, extroversion, sensitivity and independence.

FORMAT

The test has 187 statements expressed in the first person with three possible responses.

EXAMPLE

I like watching football matches:

A. Yes

B. Sometimes

C. No

DURATION OF TEST

No specific time limit, between 30 and 40 minutes.

HOW YOU SCORE

Each answer has a coefficient that is credited or debited in relation to a particular tendency. Thus for the statement above, a 'Yes' increases your extroversion level by one point, 'No' reduces it and 'Sometimes' increases your moderation score.

POINTS TO WATCH

Avoid responding with 'Sometimes' too often. You will be seen as someone with a weak personality, or they may think you are not prepared to show your true colours.

Look out for traps

All personality tests are based on the same principles. They differ less in presentation than in the character traits, tendencies and motivation aspects that they set out to explore. Occasionally questions are confusing, highly personal or downright ambiguous. It is difficult to know how to respond to enhance your profile when faced with questions such as 'Do you suffer from insomnia?', 'Do you like football?' or 'Do you prefer historical novels or science fiction?' which are supposed to measure your degree of adaptability, sociability, etc.

The most important thing is to play the game. You are dealing with professionals so don't think you are a cut above!

Most of these questionnaires contain little traps. Certain questions obviously do not present the candidate in a positive light, (e.g. 'Are you a bad loser?', 'As a child, did you steal money from your mother's purse?' or 'Do you have tantrums?' But if you say 'No' each time, then inevitably (it has been statistically proven) you must be cheating.

The best thing (or the least bad) is to tell the truth, whilst nevertheless trying to avoid accumulating answers that will automatically put you into the 'high risk' category.

PERSONALITY TESTS (3) — BONNARDEL'S BV 16 AND BV 17

Aptitude tests are used by one in four companies for recruiting executives, in conjunction with an intelligence test such as one of those given on pages 17–19. The most widely used in this category are Bonnardel's BV 16 and BV 17 Tests (BV 17 is the more difficult version).

AIM

To evaluate intelligence from the point of view of understanding ideas, ability to analyse, objectivity and ability to make pertinent judgements.

FORMAT

A quotation is given, followed by six sentences. You are asked to tick the two sentences that, in your opinion, seem to reflect most accurately (or at least be closest to) the meaning of the quotation. There are 11 quotations in all.

EXAMPLE

Tick the two sentences that are the most similar to the following statement:

'Intelligence would not go far if conscience were not a constant companion.'

    A.   Many actions are carried out without thinking.

    B.   An intelligent person should always act in accordance with his conscience.

    C.   In the realms of the unconscious there is no intelligence.

    D.   Few actions are accomplished without intelligence.

    E.   Man is as sensitive as he is rational.

    F.   Man is more circumspect in his actions than in his thoughts.

DURATION OF TEST

15 minutes only.

POINTS TO WATCH

Designed in the early 1950s, the BV 16 and BV 17 presuppose some objectivity in the meanings expressed, a sort of common sense. Since that time, concepts have changed so that words do not have exactly the same meaning. It is therefore extremely difficult to give the right answers.

HOW YOU SCORE

Each sentence has a score of between +2 (the two sentences that are considered to be the closest to the meaning of the statement given) and −2 (the two that are the least similar in meaning). Your score is then compared to average scores. Thus in the case of the example given above, the answers C and E put you above average; B and D would yield an average score and if you picked A and F you would be below average.

PERSONALITY TESTS (4) – THE IPS TEST

The Inventory of Personality for Sales Personnel (IPS) test is used only for the recruitment of sales personnel. About 9 per cent of agencies and companies use it.

AIM

To assess a candidate's suitability for sales work, by evaluating nine personality traits: activity, fighting spirit, dominance, understanding, sociability, self-control, adaptability, tolerance in frustrating circumstances and confidence.

FORMAT

The test presents 87 situations from everyday life, which involve a problem of some kind. You are given a choice of three possible solutions.

EXAMPLE

Below is an example of an embarrassing situation for which several courses of action are suggested. You must choose only one answer, the one that immediately strikes you as the most probable course of action.

James is in a department store when he sees a shoplifter stealing something. What does he do?

A. Tells the shop assistant.

B. Nothing, it's none of his business.

C. Makes it obvious to the shoplifter that he has seen him take something.

DURATION OF TEST

About 30 minutes.

HOW YOU SCORE

Each answer increases or reduces a certain tendency. For example, in the case of the question cited above the answer A increases your 'activity' score, B decreases it, and C increases your 'dominance' rating.

POINTS TO WATCH

Even if you are not looking for a sales-oriented job, do not overlook this test.

Although it was originally designed to recruit sales assistants and sales representatives, it has often been used to recruit other types of staff, including executives, engineers and technicians.

COMPUTERISED QUESTIONNAIRES (1) — THE PAPI

Due to their ease of presentation and analysis, the use of computerised tests has become increasingly widespread to cope with the ever-increasing number of candidates.

The PAPI test from the PA Consulting Group is doubtless the most widely used computerised test at the moment. It is equally popular with individual head-hunters and the selection boards of multinational companies.

Problems with computerised tests

Computerised tests have three inherent problems for recruitment specialists. Firstly, there is the potential anxiety factor linked to the use of computers. Candidates faced with a computer screen do not respond in the same way as they do when given a sheet of paper. They may be more spontaneous in front of a computer if they are used to using one but the opposite may also be true.

Secondly, allowances need to be made for new computer technology variables, such as reaction time, which are not scientifically valid.

Thirdly, the software used in certain tests will adapt the questions according to candidates' responses. In other words, the test becomes infinitely variable.

To alleviate these problems there are some tests that can be taken in two versions, either on screen or on paper. If this is the case, you can request whichever suits you best.

AIM

To identify 20 personality traits, including ability to delegate, ability to work alone, sociability, productivity, decision-making ability, etc., and combine them to create a behavioural profile.

FORMAT

The test consists of 45 pairs of sentences from each of which you choose the one that seems to you to be the most appropriate description of your own behaviour.

EXAMPLE

In each group of two statements choose the one which best describes you or your feelings.

> **A.** 1. I work a lot.
>   2. I make friends easily.
>
> **B.** 1. I make decisions quickly.
>   2. I like talking about what I've done.

DURATION OF TEST

There is no strict limit, but it should take between 10 and 20 minutes. If you spend more time than that they will question your ability to make decisions.

POINTS TO WATCH

You can argue your point of view. The way you handle your own results and your reactions to any comments the recruiter makes are part and parcel of the test.

HOW YOU SCORE

Each answer has a positive or negative effect (1 point either way) on a personality trait or tendency. Hence for the questions above:

'I work a lot' increases your productivity score.

'I make friends easily' increases your sociability rating.

'I make decisions quickly' indicates your ability to make decisions.

And, obviously, 'I like talking about what I've done' indicates your need to be the centre of attention.

COMPUTERISED QUESTIONNAIRES (2) – SIGMUND'S POTENTIAL

Our second example of a computerised questionnaire is Sigmund's Potential, which is used by 4 per cent of recruitment services and also many large companies.

AIM

To identify and examine 38 personality traits, including independence, team spirit, leadership, respect for hierarchy and tradition, negotiating skills, ease of contact with others, management skills, willingness to take risks, capacity to cope with failure, and even your ability to conform with the requirements of the test you are taking.

FORMAT

It consists of 450 questions, each with a response time in relation to the complexity of the question and the time required to read it.

EXAMPLE

What do you think of this statement?

'One can't instigate action without neglecting a great many factors.' (10 seconds)

A. Very true

B. True

C. It's not that simple

D. False

DURATION OF TEST

Unlimited, but it should take about 1 hour.

POINTS TO WATCH

It is impossible to change an answer and the time given for your answers is often very short. Furthermore, the screen often puts up distracting messages, such as: 'I think you are in need of a short rest', or 'I sense a certain lack of self-awareness in your answers'. Do not let them put you off balance.

HOW YOU SCORE

Each answer impacts on a personality trait's rating in a positive or negative way. For example, in the case of the example, the answer 'Very true' increases your rating in willingness to take risks; 'False' decreases your leadership score.

PROJECTIVE TESTS (1) – RORSCHACH'S INK BLOT TEST

Projective tests are also personality tests but, unlike the computerised questionnaires, they ask you to interpret or construct something in order to bring out your character and to express your tendencies. They are used by 20.5 per cent of all big companies and by recruitment agencies. One of the most popular and certainly the most famous is Rorschach's Ink Blot Test, designed in 1921 by Hermann Rorschach, a Swiss psychiatrist, which is used by 6 per cent of agencies; many companies use it for recruiting their most senior staff.

AIM

To paint a complete picture of the candidate's personality in all its dimensions: mental, emotional and instinctive.

FORMAT

The test consists of ten pictures of ink blots, some of which are black, others are coloured. They are numbered from I to 10 and presented in that order. Usually you are asked 'What do you see in the blot?', but sometimes the instructions are more conditional or more directive.

DURATION OF TEST

Very variable, may be up to several hours.

HOW YOU SCORE

Type of response
Your responses are marked according to two criteria; quantitative and qualitative.

For the **quantitative score** the examiner is looking at:

• The total number of responses

• The total time taken

• The time per response

For the **qualitative score** the examiner takes note of:

• The specific quality of the response; whether it is 'general' or 'detailed'

• The type of response: whether it is related to form, colour or movement

• The content of the perception, categorised as 'animal', 'human' and 'anatomical'

Number of responses
The statistical average is between 20 and 30 responses. You would be expected to give between 40 and 50 responses if you had gone on to higher education. You should aim for these norms.

A number of responses that scores very much below average (less than 15) may indicate several possible factors, including intellectual backwardness, depression, pathological problems, emotional block and an inability to co-operate.

A number of responses that is well above average (over 50) is equally suspect and may, for example, indicate a superiority complex.

Time per response
Average response time is about 45 seconds. You should not exceed this limit for each figure.

An excessively slow reaction time (more than 60 seconds) is considered to indicate a potentially serious psychological problem; too quick (less than 20 seconds) suggests a certain incoherence in one's ideas, or a lack of control over one's self-expression.

Types of interpretation
The average score for general responses (the overall interpretation of the blot) is between 7 and 10. General responses score well when they represent the right shapes, and poorly for the wrong ones. A high number (above average) of accurate general responses suggests associative intelligence, which will manifest as good organisational ability, good integration and synthesis skills. However, too many inaccurate general responses suggests a rather superficial intelligence, a tendency to generalise and a lack of critical ability.

Interpreting large areas
The average score for the interpretation of any large areas of the blot is between 15 and 21. These responses are also categorised as 'good shapes' and 'bad shapes'. A high number of good shapes in the large areas of the blot responses suggests pragmatic intelligence, a candidate who is observant and practical. However, too many bad shape responses suggests stereotyped intelligence, a lack of imagination and intellectual apathy.

Secondary scores
There is a second level of scoring, corresponding first to the interpretation of small details. On the positive side these scores suggest analytical intelligence. On the negative side they suggest a narrow-minded, petty mentality.

The secondary scores also correspond to the interpretation given to the spaces between the blots. Avoid these unless they are specifically requested or you may risk being considered to be perverse.

You will score poorly in this section if you give a partial interpretation when it is obvious that a complete response is required. Look at Figure 6 on page 92, for example, where you might identify a cat's moustache rather than its head. Don't use this technique as it is always associated with serious weaknesses, emotional inhibitions and pathological problems.

Form responses (F)

These correspond to an interpretation of the shape of the whole or part of the blot. The average percentage of form responses is between 60 and 65 per cent. Below that level, inappropriate behaviour may be suspected: anything above is a sign of overly rigid behaviour, obsession, stilted emotions and a lack of spontaneity.

Form responses are also marked + (the shapes everyone sees) and − (those which few people perceive). There is a margin of 10 to 20 per cent allowed for F− responses.

Colour responses (C)

These are categorised as C (pure colour), FC (form colour), CF (colour form). Responses of the C type (for example 'It's red') suggest an absence of emotional control, possible aggressive or depressive reactions. These are to be avoided at all costs.

FC type responses ('It's a red butterfly') suggest a socially adapted emotional response. These are the type of responses to aim for.

On the other hand, CF type ('It's red, like a butterfly') responses emphasise socially maladapted emotions, such as egocentricity, emotional instability and a capricious nature. Play down this type of response.

Movement responses (K)

K responses correspond to the interpretation of movement in the blot. They are split into two main categories:

- Extension movements. Take Figure 3 on page 89, for example: if you said 'It shows two men standing', this would indicate that you were a dynamic, enterprising and creative person. This is the type of response you should be aiming for, whilst moderating the underlying aggression of the image.

- Flexion. Looking at the same blot you might say 'It shows two men kneeling'. This is the response of introverts, people who are somewhat passive. However you can occasionally go for this type of response (not too often) as it also suggests qualities associated with patience.

However, K responses are best avoided completely when they involve animals or objects. Such responses are always interpreted as indicating repressed aggression and internal conflicts.

Shading

Shading is also taken into account for the overall scoring: it is linked with colour responses, the perception of grey and shades of grey, and the contrast of light and dark.

Responses to the shading characteristics of the blot are supposed to indicate a state of depression and should be avoided. Shading/form responses (with the shading dominant) are a sign of over-suggestibility and should also be avoided.

Form/shading responses (with the form dominant) are considered to indicate an inferiority complex if there is any hint of relief or perspective (for example, 'It's a reflection in a lake'); powerful emotional frustrations are indicated if texture is suggested ('It's furry', or 'It's made of snow'). Do not overuse this type of comment.

The light/dark relationship is a particular type of shading, linked to the perception of blocks of black with unpleasant overtones. It may indicate anxiety (as in responses such as 'It's dirty snow', 'It's a skull'); depression ('It looks like burnt-out ruins, or a petrified forest...') or aggression ('There's a storm threatening', 'I can see a black ghost'). You should eliminate this type of response altogether.

Human responses (H)

These are frequently found in the interpretation: 10–20 per cent of male responses are 'human', and 15–30 per cent of females. However, if you score in excess of these norms, you will be suspected of neurosis or family conflicts during childhood.

H responses are assessed in three ways:

- H (a human figure in its entirety)

- Hd (a partial human being)

- H/Hd for para-human shapes, either whole or partial (ghost, witch, angel, demon, portrait, etc.)

The normal ratio of H to Hd is 2 to 1. An inverse proportion (2Hd to 1H) suggests a lack of intelligence or a very anxious personality.

H and Hd type responses are to be avoided as much as possible. They are a sign of emotional immaturity and childish reactions.

RORSCHACH'S TYPOLOGY

The ratio of K (movement) to C (colour) responses highlights four character types:

K is greater than C – the introvert

- Intellectual discrimination
- Personal productivity
- Predominance of internal life
- Constancy of emotions
- Poor adaptation to reality
- Deeply felt rather than broadly applied sympathies
- Measured conduct
- Clumsiness

C is greater than K – the extrovert

- Stereotyped intelligence
- Ease of reproduction
- Predominance of external life
- Unstable emotions
- Adapts easily to reality
- Broadly applied rather than deeply felt sympathies
- Impulsiveness

- Adeptness

K and C are equal and in excess of three – the ambivalent type

- Alternates between phases of achievement and internalisation

- Ambivalence in behaviour and emotions, swinging between impulsiveness and restraint

- Indecisiveness combined with behaviour that is sometimes highly efficient and at other times quite the opposite

Where the ratio of K to C = 0 : 0 or 1 : 1

- Restraint of personality

- Low energy levels

- Internalised emotions

- Low level of personal productivity

- Efficient in activities where there is no personal involvement

'Animal' responses: A

A responses account for 25 to 50 per cent of the questions and are put into three categories: A (for the whole animal), Ad (for a part), A/Ad for a quasi-animal, whether whole or only partially shown (monster, mythical creature, cartoon...).

A score of less than 30 per cent of type A responses (which includes all the A-related categories) would indicate an overactive imagination, incoherent thinking or an antisocial personality.

A score of more than 60 per cent of type A responses suggests childish thought patterns, a lack of culture or an overly rigid mindset.

'Anatomy' responses: Anat

Such responses would include identifying skeletons, foetuses, lungs, etc. Unless you are a medic or a paramedic you should avoid more than one or two Anat responses. If you give more than this, your responses will be interpreted as signs of an inferiority complex, worries about health or veiled sexual problems such as feelings of guilt and shame.

Beware

Some responses should be avoided at all costs as they are interpreted as signs of pathological tendencies:

- Masks and clothing: these may be taken as signs of concealment or perversion

- Drinks: alcoholic tendencies

- An open mouth: oral fixation

- Statues, drawings and caricatures: detachment from reality

- Combat, weapons, etc: potential violence

- The elements (air, fire, water and earth): infantile tendencies and acute neurosis

- Fragments of dirt, mud, droppings, etc: obsessive neuroses

- Bacteria and rotting flesh: psychological problems

- Rotten trees, charred wood, black smoke, etc.: suicidal tendencies

- Responses to do with the symmetry, number or position of the blots: loss of sense of reality.

Secondary content responses

These are responses mainly to do with sex, blood, objects, plants, geography, nature and food and drink. They are best avoided wherever possible.

Sex responses are unusual, even though certain figures are highly suggestive (see Figures 2, 4, 6 and 7 on pages 88, 90, 92, 93). To stay within the accepted norm, only one sex response is possible (Figure 6).

Blood responses, which as well as blood include fire, lava etc., hint at a lack of emotional control or potential aggressiveness.

Object responses (particularly pointed objects, such as weapons and tongs, and hollow objects, such as vases and urns) are considered to be signs of infantile tendencies (except in the case of related technical professions) or of sexual obsessions.

Plant responses (plants, trees, seaweed, etc.) and nature responses (rocks, lakes, mountains, etc.) suggest highly neurotic infantile tendencies.

Geographical responses (islands, countries, etc.) are considered to be the expression of an inferiority complex or escapism.

Food and drink responses are taken to be indicative of inner distress or anxiety.

COMPLEMENTARY SCORING

Three other factors are taken into account when evaluating your results:

The banality or originality of the responses
Banal or stereotyped responses are those that are given by one in three people according to Rorschach; original responses are given by only one per cent. Your ratio of original to stereotyped responses should be 3 to 7. Below this norm you are considered to be highly conformist, whilst above it you are seriously maladjusted.

The shock response
The examiner considers that there is a shock, or excessive, reaction to a figure when he picks up five of the following signs:

- An exclamation of approval or disapproval such as 'Yuck', 'Phew', 'Oh really…'

- Criticism or self-criticism expressed in remarks such as 'Oh my God', 'That's lovely', or 'It looks a bit rude'

- Anxious handling of the figure, wringing of hands, furrowing of brows, hesitation, prolonged silences, signs of denial ('This really isn't my scene', 'This is killing me…')

- Prolonged reflection on one particular figure

- Marked increase in the rate of responses

- Significant decrease in the quality of responses

- Absence of 'colour' responses to the coloured figures (particularly Figure 8)

- Absence of expected common responses to certain figures (for example, no stereotyped responses to Figures 3, 5 and 8)

- Escape into the spaces in the blot or to the edges

- Responses expressing personal problems

Refusal
A refusal is when you can't give an interpretation. When you dry up the examiner encourages you. If you persist in refusing, it is taken to be a very bad sign. According to Rorschach, 'normal' people never refuse to have a go.

The most commonly refused figures are 9, 7, 6 and 4, in that order.

HOW TO INTERPRET THE BLOTS

You can prepare your responses but do not attempt to learn them off by heart. Psychologists are not idiots and they are well used to pretence, so an 'ideal' pattern of response would make a mockery of your test. Your interpretation of the blots should therefore show a certain degree of spontaneity. This is especially important as once the test has ended the examiner will refer back to each and every one of your responses: you will be questioned as to your reasons, whether they were inspired by shape or colour and so on.

Normally the interpretation of a blot is done in a certain order. First of all you should interpret the blot as a whole (general responses), then some of the important sections of detail, followed by some of the smaller details. Finally, and only if asked, you can interpret a detail within the non-coloured or blank section.

In the following pages you will find some of the general responses for each figure as well as some of the main details taken from those which occur the most frequently.

Top tips for success

1. Be careful not to react or comment in any way when you are shown the figures.

2. Do not say you can't (or won't) interpret a figure.

3. Give your general responses before interpreting the detailed sections.

4. Interpret the coloured sections by giving form/colour responses ('It's a red butterfly') rather than colour/form ('It's red, rather like a butterfly').

5. Do not give pure colour responses, such as 'It's red', 'It's blue', 'It's all pink,' or similar. Say 'It looks like blood' or 'It's a fire' for the red, 'I can see a lake' or 'It's the sky' for blue, etc.

6. Do not interpret the small details or the blanks unless requested.

7. Give 'human' or 'animal' responses in movement rather than 'object' or fixed responses.

8. Avoid wherever possible sexual (except Figure 6), anatomy, geography, plant, nature and food responses or responses that refer to a blurred view (clouds, smoke, etc.).

9. Avoid giving the same responses for several figures even if they do look alike.

10. Do not refer to your personal life, either present or past.

Figure 1

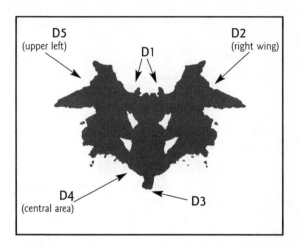

General responses

Stereotyped: butterfly or bat (the most popular), eagle, angel, badge, crab, leaf, flea, bird

Original: bee, coat of arms, duck, cocoon, grotto, wasp, lobster

Detailed responses

D1 stereotyped: antennae, horns, fingers, hands, tongs
D1 original: puppet, butterfly, thumb, rock
D2 stereotyped: acrobat, wings, angel, dancer, bird, Pegasus
D2 original: rabbit, cloud, woodpecker (side view)
D3 stereotyped: legs, totem, statue, vase
D3 original: crocodile, robot, spaceship, violin
D4 stereotyped: beetle, woman, gorilla, statue, cello
D4 original: baboon, crown, monument, vase, viola
D5 stereotyped: eagle, wings, rook, bird, sphinx
D5 original: duck, cliff, weather vane, nest, cloud, rock

Figure 2

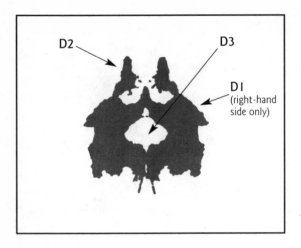

General responses
Stereotyped: dancers, ornament, bear, statues
Original: (abstract) art, emblem, gorillas, grotto, chickens, bookends, torches, volcano

Detailed responses
D1 stereotyped: bear, dog, elephant, lamb
D1 original: animal, rock, cloud
D2 stereotyped: bonnet, hat, puppet, bird, seal, torch
D2 original: angel, snail, rabbit, walrus, chicken
D3 stereotyped: crab, butterfly, painting
D3 original: sea anemone, coral, fan, flower, skate (fish)

Figure 3

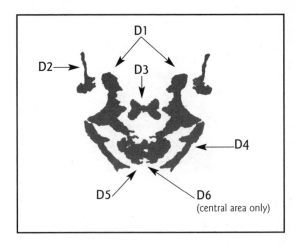

General responses
Stereotyped: animals, human figures, birds
Original: badge, chandelier, drinking vessel, logo, emblem

Detailed responses
D1 stereotyped: ostrich, human figures, sheep, dolls
D1 original: boat hull, radio, vase
D2 stereotyped: animal, pan, hat, puppet, monkey
D2 original: amoeba, chandelier, coral, hook, stomach, guitar, robot
D3 stereotyped: bow tie, lungs, ribbon
D3 original: wing, fossil, wasp, halter, sunglasses, bra
D4 stereotyped: leg, paw, fish, shark
D4 original: baton, bomb, log, arrow, rocket, torpedo
D5 stereotyped: cauldron, crab, nest, baskets, rock(s)
D5 original: coal, gate, drum, vertebra
D6 stereotyped: ribs, bones, skeleton
D6 original: crab, lamp, stone, sandpit

Figure 4

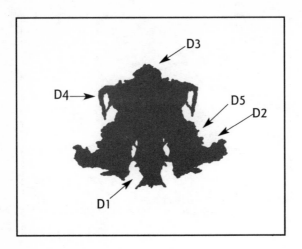

General responses

Stereotyped: human, humanoid, sea animal, tree, bush, gorilla, plant, rug

Original: seaweed, squid, kite, bell, sponge, frog, dress

Detailed responses

D1 stereotyped: bush, caterpillar, insect, stool

D1 original: fire hydrant, snail, tail

D2 stereotyped: shoe, foot

D2 original: wing, cliff, cloud, sphinx, statue

D3 stereotyped: blossom, shell, head (of a cat, owl or monkey, etc.)

D3 original: beret, mushroom, cabbage, fan, cockle, vagina

D4 stereotyped: branch, claw, lizard, diver, snake, stalactite

D4 original: eel, tail, root, elephant's trunk

D5 stereotyped: boot, leg, foot

D5 original: wing, shoe, rudder, Italy

Figure 5

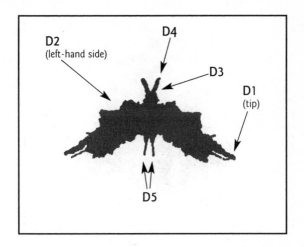

General responses

Stereotyped: butterfly, bat (the most popular), dancer, Dracula, bird, vampire, vulture

Original: eagle, angel, aeroplane, duck, rook, shawl, oyster, moustache, flea, spaceship

Detailed responses

D1 stereotyped: leg, bone, reptile head

D1 original: baton, branch, arm, log, muscle, root

D2 stereotyped: bushes, human figure lying down, rock, profile of human head

D2 original: seaweed, blanket, fan, cloud, sleeping bag

D3 stereotyped: head of animal (viewed from front), human head wearing mask

D3 original: antennae, scissors, catapult, claws, wishbone

D4 stereotyped: swans, bird's feet, claws

D4 original: vacuum cleaner, beak, paws, tails

D5 stereotyped: root, reptile's head

D5 original: box spanner, legs, paws, head (of bird, or cartoon figure)

Figure 6

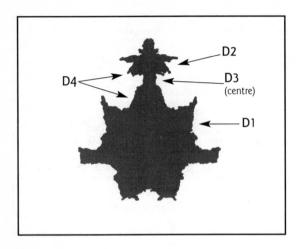

General responses
Stereotyped: animal, animal skin, rug, fur
Original: aeroplane, leaf, rudder, guitar, cello

Detailed responses
D1 stereotyped: boat, blanket, leaf, coat, statue, rug
D1 original: baby's bottle, buckle, sponge, clouds, gate, urn
D2 stereotyped: alligator, candle, street lamp, lamppost, totem pole
D2 original: eel, nail, sword, penis, reptile
D3 stereotyped: lighted match, crucifix, fan, goose, statue, totem pole
D3 original: tree, aeroplane, rocket, fly, butterfly
D4 stereotyped: cross, ghost, scarecrow, fountain, lighthouse, plant, totem pole
D4 original: tree, aeroplane, insect (with wings), bird, statue

Figure 7

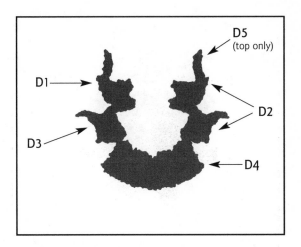

General responses
Stereotyped: foodstuffs (coated or fried), canyon, elves, humans, clouds, port
Original: swing, necklace, crown, prawns, horseshoe, reef, stool

Detailed responses
D1 stereotyped: prawn, cliff, rabbit, statue
D1 original: cactus, commode, ladle, fist (with finger outstretched)
D2 stereotyped: angel, snowman, rabbit, dwarf, cloud(s)
D2 original: lamb, bush, hill, mountain
D3 stereotyped: mask, head (of animal, cartoon figure or toy)
D3 original: candy floss, chopper, cloud, rock, statue
D4 stereotyped: pelvis, cloud(s), butterfly, rock
D4 original: kite, cushions, hang-glider, bow tie, bookends
D5 stereotyped: knife blade, feather
D5 original: caterpillar, head-dress, finger, claws, comb, sabre, stalagmite

Figure 8

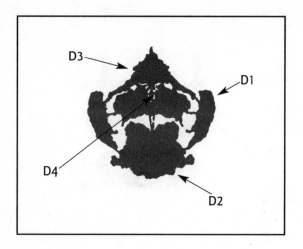

General responses
Stereotyped: coat of arms, art (abstract), sailing boat (viewed from front or rear), chandelier, chalice, fountain, merry-go-round
Original: badge, cage (bird), kite, circus big top, flag, pagoda

Detailed responses
D1 stereotyped: beaver, bear, cat, dog, lion, mouse, rat, wolf
D1 original: iguana, lizard, petal, blood
D2 stereotyped: flower, ice cream, lava, butterfly
D2 original: coral, cake, pot, rug
D3 stereotyped: frog, mountains, roots, spaceship
D3 original: spider, aeroplane, boomerang, robot, vine
D4 stereotyped: flag, water, lake, butterfly, material
D4 original: bat, cloud(s), bird, sails (boat)

Figure 9

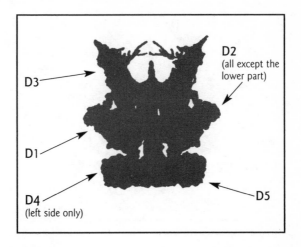

General responses
Stereotyped: bouquet of flowers, head-dress, explosion, leaves,
    fountain, garden
Original: anchor, cactus, hat, decoration, spaceship

Detailed responses
D1 stereotyped: bush, leaves, grass, landscape
D1 original: coral, sponge, fern, cloud, plant
D2 stereotyped: anchor, bowl, flower, mask, vase
D2 original: badge, hat, fountain, garden, ornament
D3 stereotyped: animal, clown, devil, flower, toy, sand, witch
D3 original: wing, carrot, dragon, lobster, statue, torch
D4 stereotyped: candy floss, raspberry, apple
D4 original: sponge, strawberry, mask, rock
D5 stereotyped: balloons, two babies, cloud, four apples
D5 original: strawberries, powder puff, marshmallows

Figure 10

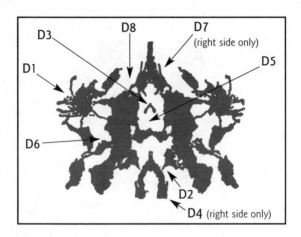

General responses
Stereotyped: aquarium, insects, garden in bloom, painting (modern)
Original: bacteria, chandelier, fireworks, kaleidoscope, plants

Detailed responses
D1 stereotyped: amoeba, spider, crab, octopus, scorpion
D1 original: seaweed, earring, coral, dragon, lobster, pompom
D2 stereotyped: dog, flower, lion, fried egg
D2 original: cat, insect, seal
D3 stereotyped: breastbone, cherries
D3 original: earphones, floats, door knocker, spaceship
D4 stereotyped: eels, caterpillar, snake
D4 original: boot, horn, snail
D5 stereotyped: gorillas, humanoids, bridge
D5 original: ducks, bagpipes, nest, pipes, bra
D6 stereotyped: cockroach, deer, crab, ant, grasshopper
D6 original: seaweed, cocoon, seed, claw, praying mantis
D7 stereotyped: dragon, ant, insect, monster
D7 original: bee, crab, elf, unicorn, dwarf, parrot, vermin, rodent
D8 stereotyped: caterpillar, coral, humanoid, mummy, mermaid
D8 original: bacon, sea horse, intestine, cloud

PROJECTIVE TESTS (2) – MURRAY'S PICTURE TEST

One of the best-known projective tests is the Thematic Apperception Test (TAT), which was designed in the 1930s by Henry A Murray, an American psychologist. Along with the Rorschach Ink Blot Test (see page 76), it is one of the most popular image tests in the world.

It is also probably the most controversial in that there is a high degree of subjectivity in the interpretation of the results. Nevertheless, it is still used frequently by recruitment agencies for selecting executives.

AIM

The TAT claims to make a complete psychological diagnosis (conscious and unconscious) of the candidate's personality, what Murray called 'an X-ray of one's deepest self'. It was designed to identify motivating factors and feelings (aggression, self-aggression, domination, submission, eroticism, etc.), as well as outside pressures and relationships with others.

FORMAT

The original American version of the test has 31 pictures. The example we use here describes 16 of them. Each one represents an image, except number 16, which is blank. Some of the figures are unisex, others feminine or masculine. The black and white pictures include drawings, photographs and copies of paintings or engravings.

Candidates are instructed to 'interpret' the pictures. This interpretation, according to Murray, means that they 'perceive the intrigue or the dramatic structure within each picture.' For the blank picture, number 16, candidates are expected to conjure up their own mental picture before telling the story.

The test is usually presented in two sessions, two days apart. Candidates are given 13 or 14 figures, with Murray's instructions:

'This is a test of your imaginative creativity. You will be shown a picture and, using it as a prompt, I want you to invent a story. What is going on between the various individuals in the image? What has happened to them? What are their thoughts and their feelings at this moment? What is going to happen next?

Do your best. Give free rein to your imagination as a story teller; make the story as long and as detailed as you like.'

All the candidates' stories are recorded in their entirety. At the end of each session, the examiner questions the candidates as to the source of their inspiration.

DURATION OF TEST

There is no precise limit, but the test will last between 1 and 2 hours, giving about five minutes to tell each story. If you exceed this, you will not be stopped but you will be informed afterwards.

ANALYSIS OF RESULTS

Murray recommended two types of analysis: firstly, of the form of the story itself and secondly, an analysis of the content. In each story he was looking for:

- A protagonist, the hero with whom the candidate identifies by transferring to him his own feelings and motivations

- Secondary characters on whom the candidate projects his or her own family or social relationships (whether real or imagined)

Today, however, other additional analysis techniques are used, particularly psychoanalytical techniques.

Analysis based on form
The form analysis aims to detect information on your type and degree of intelligence: critical or literary abilities, intuition, sense of reality, organisation of thoughts, coherence of ideas and any possible pathological tendencies.

You will be assessed according to:

- Your understanding of instructions

- Your degree of co-operation

- Your perception of the images

- Your ability to tell stories as opposed to simply interpreting information

- The way you construct the stories: their coherence and verisimilitude, pertinence to the image, style, richness of detail

- The language you use: quality of vocabulary and expression, syntax, predominance of certain categories of words (verbs, adjectives, etc.)

Analysis of content
Murray considered the content in five ways:

- The search for a central character for each story: the hero. Sometimes it may be necessary to distinguish between a principal and a secondary hero. The feelings and the actions of the hero are taken to represent the real feelings and motivations of the candidate.

- The forces exerted on the hero by his entourage: there may be positive or negative influences evident in the feelings and actions with which the candidate imbues the secondary characters.

- The action and the outcome of the story: the hero's reactions in the situation imagined by the candidate, the way in which this situation evolves towards its end, the way in which the end occurs and finally the nature of the outcome itself.

- Analysis of the theme of the story: its originality, dramatic context and psychological richness.

- Interests and feelings expressed; the positive or negative attitudes of the hero towards the people who resemble him or her (age, gender, etc.), and in relation to the people of the opposite sex (desire/disgust) or to older people (parental figures).

THE PICTURES

They have an obvious visible content as well as a hidden, suggested content. You should construct your story in the light of both of these aspects. Most psychologists agree on the manifest and latent material in each picture. These agreed versions are described below.

Picture 1

Manifest content
A young boy is seated with his elbows on the table and a violin and bow in front of him. He seems to be looking at them with a morose or thoughtful air.

Latent content
Suggests the image of a child faced with an adult object. This could give signs of your ability to react when faced with a difficult or an immediate impossibility. Typical stories are usually constructed around the following themes: child refusing to play the violin, child dreaming of a glorious future, child forced to play and threatened with punishment, happy child wanting to own a violin, etc.

Picture 2

Manifest content
A country scene with meadows, hills, houses and trees. In the foreground on the right there is a peasant woman leaning against a tree with her arms crossed; on the left stands another young woman, obviously a town-dweller, holding some books. In the

Top tips for success

1. Do not simply describe what you see, but do not let your imagination run riot either. Your story must stick to the illustration and remain within the bounds of possibility. Keep to simple scenarios without being downright boring.

2. Do choose a positive hero who is sociable, enterprising, responsible and optimistic; make your hero of the same sex and, wherever possible, about the same age as you.

3. Do tell positive stories (with a happy ending) even if certain images are designed to suggest a dramatic atmosphere. Avoid catastrophic or sad settings (destitution, incurable disease, hopeless situations, etc.), scenarios redolent of defeat (abandonment, surrender, flight, etc.) or aggression (persecution, desire for power), obsession (cleanliness, saving money, arranging objects in order) or sex (eroticism in the relationships, crude expressions).

4. Do abstain from any political or religious references.

5. Do not dramatise or idealise. Don't describe anything as though viewed through rose-coloured spectacles.

6. Do not allow the roles to overlap. Your characters must be easy to identify and to follow through the story.

7. Do not make sudden changes of direction in your narration. Your story must flow logically without flashbacks or theatrical effects.

8. Do keep your prose calm. Avoid adding exclamations, over-expressive mimicry, hand gestures, etc. or using irony, sarcasm, derision or taking the examiner into your confidence (asking direct questions or adding little asides for the reader, etc.).

9. Do avoid personal or autobiographical references. Do not tell your life story; keep yourself out of the story.

10. Afterwards, do not deny having said something when the examiner shows a particular interest in some part of your story.

middle there is the back view of a bare-chested man, working with a horse.

Latent content
Suggests the Oedipus father–mother–daughter triangle with opposition between mother–daughter, town–country, intellectual–manual. Could indicate your relationship with your parents and any possible family conflicts.

Picture 3

Manifest content
An individual (gender and age unknown), sprawled out on the ground, with their right arm and head resting on a bench. On the ground there is a blurred object.

Latent content
Suggests a depressing situation. May reveal something of your reactions in the face of loss. The most frequent themes offered are momentary sadness, punishment, suicide, physical exhaustion, guilt, despair, poverty and prison.

Picture 4

Manifest content
A woman with her arms round a man who is looking away. In the background there is another lightly clad woman, sitting down on a sofa with her head bowed.

Latent content
Suggests a conflict between a couple. Will reveal your bias (aggression/tenderness) in this type of conflict.

Many candidates do not notice the second woman and so fail to include her in their narrative.

Picture 5

Manifest content
Shows part of a room. In the foreground on the right is a table, with a lamp and a vase of flowers; on the left is a middle-aged woman with her hand on the door handle, looking inside.

Latent content
Suggests the concern of a mother figure. Will reveal your ability to exercise self-control.

Picture 6 (for men)

Manifest content
An elderly woman is standing near a window, looking away. Directly in front of her is a man with his eyes cast down, looking worried; he is wearing an overcoat and carrying a hat.

Latent content
Suggests a difficult mother–son relationship. Could expose an Oedipus complex.

Picture 6 (for women)

Manifest content
A young woman is sitting on a sofa, turning towards a man who is leaning towards her.

Latent content
Suggests a situation where two people are becoming increasingly familiar (physical closeness of the one to the other) but in difficult circumstances (they are separated by the sofa). The two people are often seen as being an unmarried couple: this is a tell-tale sign of your attitudes towards desire and forbidden fruits.

Picture 7 (for men)

Manifest content
Shows the top half of two men, seated side by side. One of the two, the older, is turned towards the other, a young man who is sulking and appears to be looking into the distance.

Latent content
Suggests disagreement in a father–son relationship. Will reveal your bias (reconciliation/opposition) faced with this type of discord.

Picture 7 (for women)

Manifest content
A woman is sitting on a sofa with a book in her hand, leaning dreamily towards a little girl hugging a doll.

Latent content
Suggests the mother–daughter relationship in a context of identification and rivalry. Will reveal your feelings towards the maternal image and to motherhood.

Picture 8

Manifest content
A bare-chested man is lying down on a bed: two men are leaning over him with an instrument. In the foreground on the left is a boy on his own with his back to the scene, and on the right-hand side there is a shotgun.

Latent content
Suggests a scene of aggression between adults and an adolescent. Will reveal your destructive impulses and any fears of impotence.

Picture 9 (for men)

Manifest content
Four men, three of whom seem to be asleep, are lying down on the grass. Only two of their faces are visible, and these are half-hidden by their hats.

Latent content
Suggests a strong, virile sense of brotherhood. The boy who is not asleep is usually seen to be opposed to the others. Will indicate ability to integrate into a group and whether you have any potential homosexual impulses. This picture is rarely used.

Picture 9 (for women)

Manifest content
A young woman stands behind a tree, holding a magazine and another (indiscernible) object in her left hand. She is surreptitiously

watching another young woman running along the bank, holding up the skirt of her low-necked evening dress with one hand.

Latent content
Suggests a situation of female rivalry in a dramatic situation. Will reveal your position towards dominating/being dominated.

Picture 10

Manifest content
A young woman has her head and left hand on the chest of a tall man. Only their faces and her hand are clearly visible.

Latent content
Suggests a 'couple' situation. The stories told are generally on the following themes: harmony, separation, meeting after a separation, comforting, advice and reconciliation.

Picture 11

Manifest content
A chaotic landscape on a hillside is shown. In the background there seems to be a reptile coming out of a crack in the rock. In the foreground there is a figure, perhaps a man, driving cattle towards a bridge through a rocky passage.

Latent content
Suggests a difficult and stressful situation. Will reveal your defence mechanisms when faced with stress.

Picture 13

Manifest content
A woman, bare from the waist up, is lying on a bed, and a man stands in the foreground with his arm in front of his face.

Latent content
Suggests sex-related problems. Will reveal your sexuality and your aggression as a partner within a couple.

Picture 14

Manifest content
A young boy is sitting on the doorstep of a dilapidated shed.

Latent content
Suggests one's capacity for solitude. Will reveal your potential for independent action. This figure is not always presented.

Picture 15

Manifest content
Shows a fantasy image of a house in the snow or a boat in a storm with whirlpools, ghosts, etc.

Latent content
Suggests phobias. Will reveal your attractions/aversions.

Picture 16

Manifest content
Shows a blank page. You make up your own image and narrative.

Latent content
Will show up any narcissistic tendencies and reveal what you like best (people and things), and your ability to order them as well as how you relate to them.

PROJECTIVE TESTS (3) – ROSENWEIG'S CARTOON TEST

Rosenweig's PF, better known as Rosenweig's Cartoon Test, was designed in 1948 by Rosenzweig, an American psychologist. It is frequently used by recruitment agencies and selection boards, mainly because of its precise objective and attractive presentation but also because several candidates can be examined at the same time. It is a popular test for recruiting psychologists.

AIM

To evaluate your reactions to the stresses of everyday life (the strengths and weaknesses of your ego, your ability to overcome obstacles, take responsibility, and so on).

FORMAT

You are given a booklet of illustrations representing 24 frustrating situations, each one a stylised drawing (faces are left blank so as not to influence responses). Instructions are given as follows:

> In each of the following images in the booklet you will see two people speaking. The words of only one of the characters are given. Imagine what the other character would say and write in the bubble the first response which comes to mind.
>
> Work through the images as quickly as possible.

THE SITUATIONS

1. A car has splashed a passing pedestrian. The driver apologises; the pedestrian has to reply.

'I am so sorry we splashed your clothes; we really did our best to avoid the puddle.'

2. A guest has just broken a vase. Her hostess claims that her mother was very fond of it; the guest must respond.

'This is dreadful! That's my mother's favourite vase you have just broken.'

3. Two women are watching a show. The view of one is blocked by the hat of a woman in front of her. Her friend points this out to the woman in front; the woman who is blocking the view must respond.

4. Two people are standing outside a railway station. One apologises to the other for having caused him to miss his train because his car broke down; the other must respond.

5. A woman is complaining to a sales assistant about a recently purchased watch which is faulty. The sales assistant must respond.

6. A woman in a library is holding four books. The librarian points out to her that she can take only two books; the woman must respond.

7. A customer is speaking to a waiter in a restaurant. The waiter accuses the customer of being too fussy; the customer must respond.

8. Two men are in an office. One tells the other that he has to leave early because his girlfriend has asked him out; the other has to respond.

9. A customer has come back to a shop to collect his forgotten umbrella. It is raining outside. The employee tells him that he can't give it to him until his boss arrives in the afternoon; the customer has to respond.

10. Two men are in conversation. The first calls the second one a liar; the second one has to respond.

11. A man is woken by the phone ringing at two o'clock in the morning. The person on the other end of the line says it's a wrong number; the man who has been woken up has to respond.

12. The scene shows two men, one of whom has come back to fetch his hat. The other man explains that someone has taken it, leaving his behind instead; the first man has to respond.

13. A man is refusing to see a visitor even though he had made an appointment; the visitor has to respond.

14. Two women are standing out in the street on a windy day. One remarks that a third person they are waiting for is ten minutes late; the other woman has to respond.

15. A man and a woman are seated at a card table. The woman owns up to making a mistake which has lost them the game; her partner has to respond.

16. There has been a car accident. One of the drivers tells the other that he had no right to overtake; the other has to respond.

17. A sales assistant in a shop tells a customer that he is sorry that they don't have the article the customer wants; the customer has to respond.

18. A policeman is taking a driver to task for speeding; the driver must respond.

19. Two people discover a party to which they have not been invited. One asks the other why not; the other has to respond.

20. A man has fallen down. A second man asks him if he has hurt himself; the first one has to respond.

21. A man is standing, surrounded by suitcases, looking at a woman on the phone. The woman is saying: 'It's my aunt, she wants us to wait for her'. The man has to respond.

22. A man is returning a newspaper to another man. He apologises because his baby has torn it; the second man has to respond.

MARKING YOUR RESPONSES

Responses are marked according to two criteria: the reaction of the individual to the situation in general; and the way any aggression or frustration is directed.

Reactions to the situation

General reactions are classified in three ways:

- Centring on the obstacle, when emphasis is placed on the cause of the frustration itself

- Self-defence, when the emphasis is more on how the situation is seen to affect the individual reading the picture

- Needing a resolution, when the emphasis is more on resolving the problem.

Centring on the obstacle

The obstacle predominates when the situation of frustration is recognised and accepted as such. In this case, the emphasis placed on the obstacle may do one of three things:

- Dramatise it: 'It's a terrible nuisance', 'It's awful, I know'

- Minimise it: 'It doesn't really matter', 'Worse things happen at sea', 'We've seen worse'

- Re-appraise it: 'Let's make the best of it and ...', 'That will give us a chance to ...'

Self-defence

Self-defence occurs when the cause of the situation rather than the situation itself is brought to the fore. In this case the emphasis is on the individual's personal reaction to the obstacle:

- Passing on the responsibility to someone else, in responses such as: 'It's all your fault', 'It's not my fault'

- Taking the blame: 'It's my fault', 'I'm sorry'

- Denying that anyone is responsible: 'It's nothing to do with us', 'We can't do anything about it'

Needing a resolution
Need for a resolution is shown when the situation causing the frustration is not accepted. In this case the emphasis is on the solutions available to resolve the problem in hand:

- Expecting someone else to take action, with responses such as 'You are going to have to …', 'You owe it to me to…'

- Showing self-reliance: 'I'll sort it out', 'Leave it to me'

- Relying on time to sort things out: 'Tomorrow it will all be forgotten', 'Maybe if you come back next week,' etc.

Targets of aggression
There are three possible ways aggression may be directed:

- Outwards, on to another person

- Inwards, on to the individual feeling the aggression

- Neutrally, on to a third, uninvolved party or object

Outward responses
These are responses such as: 'It's your fault', 'You could have been a bit more careful', 'You stupid idiot'. Directed outwards, the aggression is aimed at the person considered to have caused the frustration.

Inward responses
These are responses such as: 'It's my fault', 'I'm sorry', 'I should have checked', when the aggression is aimed against oneself. It targets directly the victim of the frustration on whose shoulders the responsibility is seen to lie.

Neutral responses
These are responses such as: 'It isn't anybody's fault', 'It's nothing to do with us', ' Don't worry, it will be all right'. In these cases, the aggression is neutralised, the frustration is minimised and the responsibility for the problem is attributed neither to a third party nor to oneself.

> ### *How to conform*
> A total of 16 situations are taken into consideration to determine the degree of conformity to the group. Each response that conforms is worth one point (half a point for each part of a two-part response), with a maximum score of 16 and an average of around 9.5.
>
> You therefore need to give about ten or so normal responses if you are to indicate your good social skills and your integration to your peer group.

To achieve this, prepare your responses with the aid of the table below.

HOW YOU SCORE

Your responses are placed in the following nine categories:

	Centring on the obstacle	Self-defence	The need for resolution
Outward response	OO	O	o
Inward response	II	I	i
Neutral response	NN	N	n

Dual responses such as 'It's your fault (O), but I'll sort it out (i)', score Oi (in this case).

When a response seems to be ambiguous, you will be asked to read it to clarify the meaning.

EVALUATION OF SCORES

All the statistical studies of this test have shown that the majority of those tested gave the same type of response in 16 out of the full total of 22 situations presented.

Your responses, when compared against the statistics, will define a group conformity indicator and a profile. However, all the situations and all your responses count. The various different categories of response (OO, N, n, etc.) are separately scored and then compared with statistical averages.

The average profile is drawn up as follows:

- Outward responses (OO + O + o) = 12

- Inward responses (II + I + i) = 6

- Neutral responses (NN + N + n) = 6

- Centring on the obstacle (OO +II + NN) = 5

- Self-defence (O + I + N) = 14

- Need for resolution (o + i + n) = 5

Most of your answers should be within these norms.

PROJECTIVE TESTS (4) — KOCH AND STORA'S TREE TEST

The Tree Test was designed by the Swiss psychologist Charles Koch and adapted in France by Renée Stora. It is based on the simple idea that a drawing is always representative of the artist and that the tree is, in most cultures, the symbol for man.

It is usually used with children aged between 4 and 15, but it is also sometimes used for adults, by recruitment agencies and company selection boards.

AIM

To reveal certain personality trends: the type and level of intelligence and emotional state, the stability of the ego and whether the candidate reacts to the outside world in defence or attack mode.

FORMAT

The materials used for the test are basic: a few sheets of paper (A4), a pencil and a rubber. The instructions do not make it clear that this is a personality test. The wording of Koch's original test asked the candidate: 'Draw a fruit tree as well as you possibly can'. In Stora's later version, however, the wording ran: 'Draw a tree, any tree as long as it isn't a fir tree.' This first drawing reveals your reaction when faced with an unfamiliar environment and your capacity for self-control.

Once you have completed the first tree, you will be asked to draw a second tree, which should be different from the first. The second tree will be interpreted as revealing your ability to adapt.

Next, you will be asked to draw an 'imaginary tree, which does not exist in the real world'. This tree drawing is considered to reveal your unfulfilled desires and therefore any dilemmas you are currently facing.

Finally, your fourth tree: 'Draw a tree of any sort but do it with your eyes closed.' This drawing will reveal conflicts experienced in childhood, the consequences of which you are still dealing with.

Two parts of each drawing are interpreted:

• The structure of the tree: its roots, trunk and branches

• Any embellishments: the tree's foliage, fruit or flowers and elements of the landscape

These different factors are collated in a table. Stora's report, astonishingly, distinguishes between no less than 177 different characteristics under 15 headings, including the tree's shape, height and positioning on the page; any extraneous markings added; any shading or filling in; and the degree of freedom candidates have allowed themselves in relation to the instructions given.

EVALUATING THE RESULTS

There are several ways to evaluate the drawings:

Graphic fields
In this method a cross is overlaid on the drawing of each tree, to identify four graphics (see page 117). Each graphic field has a symbolic meaning and, when studied in relation to the cross, the drawings reveal various personality traits.

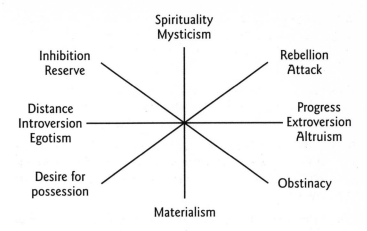

Spirituality
Mysticism

Inhibition
Reserve

Rebellion
Attack

Distance
Introversion
Egotism

Progress
Extroversion
Altruism

Desire for
possession

Obstinacy

Materialism

Taking the tree as a whole

- The top shows the predominance of the intellectual and the spiritual dimension.

- The bottom shows the predominance of the unconscious mind and the instincts, including erotico–sexual aspects.

- The centre refers to the importance of the ego, as well as the role of the conscious mind and the feelings.

- The left side is the realm of the individual's relationship with himself (introversion) and with the past.

- The right side is the realm of relationships with others (extroversion), including people in positions of authority, and of ability to project into the future.

Spatial symbolism

The system of using spatial symbolism redefines and develops the use of the cross. The schema is as follows:

Conscious
spirit

Passive zone Onlooker in life	Zone of confrontation Participant in life
Origins-regression Primal fixations	Impulse-instincts Conflicts

Mother
Past
Introversion

Father
Future
Extroversion

Unconscious
matter

Once again, by fitting the drawing into this framework the relative importance of the various components of the personality are illustrated. The schema on page 123 shows the ideal balance.

INTERPRETATION OF DRAWINGS

Statistical data reveals a certain number of constants that determine the way the drawings are interpreted.

Roots
Roots, being underground and therefore invisible, should not really be present in adult drawings. Only children, and some adults suffering from mental illness or alcoholism who are in need of some sort of anchor, draw them.

Trunk
This represents the structure of the personality, the stability of the individual's ego. Certain characteristics are significant, for example:

- A single line suggests retarded mental and emotional development.

- The absence of attachment to the ground suggests a lack of sense of reality.

- A trunk which is a tube open at the top end indicates indecision and impulsiveness.

- If the trunk widens to the left at the base, there is an excessive attachment to the past.

- If the trunk widens to the right at the base, there is some fear of authority and a lack of trust.

- A widening of the trunk at the base on both sides suggests inhibition and a lack of adaptability.

- Lumps are signs of traumatic events in the past, and personality problems.

- Nicks suggest feelings of guilt.

- If the trunk leans to the right, there is a certain weakness of character.

- If the trunk leans to the left, it is a sign of nostalgia and a lack of adaptability.

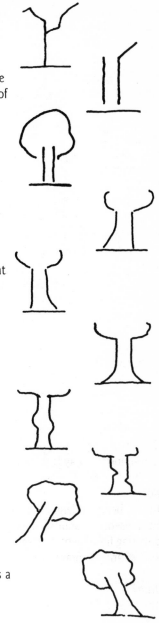

- If the trunk is linked to, and becomes, the ground, it is a sign of a lack of realism.

Branch formation
This is an expression of the way in which we have managed to adapt to the outside world through our defence and attack mechanisms. Certain formations are extremely distinctive, for example:

- A branch shaped like a tube, open at the end, shows a lack of willingness and commitment.

- Changes in width are signs of emotional instability.

- Fir-tree-type branches identify highly stereotyped thought processes.

- Pointed branches suggest aggressive, violent tendencies.

- Branches blowing to the right indicate adaptability and sociability.

- Branches blowing to the left indicate egotistical tendencies.

- Bare branches suggest a dominance of thought activity, with tendencies towards rationalisation and criticism.

- A stylised branch formation reflects emotional problems and a tendency to simplify matters.

The crown of the tree

The branch formation is often wholly or partly integrated into the crown. Certain shapes are highly significant, for example:

- A round crown with nothing in it is a sign of a character lacking imagination and easily influenced.

- A sagging crown reveals a person ruled by their feelings and lacking will-power.

- A flattened crown is a sign of feeling constrained and resigned.

- A crown leaning over to the right shows self-satisfaction and a need to be admired.

- A crown leaning over to the left shows internalisation of feelings, and inhibition in the face of problems.

- A scalloped crown is a sign of flexibility and diplomacy, sometimes even bordering on obsequiousness.

- A looped crown shows someone who makes friends easily, is easy-going and expressive.

- A decorated crown (flowers, fruit, etc.) is a sign of narcissistic tendencies such as an overwhelming need to please, sentimentality, fickleness, constant desire for affection and approval, etc.

- A scribbled crown suggests an independent personality who is productive and, at times, impulsive, with a strong desire for change.

- A shaded crown is suggestive of a malleable, easily influenced character, who may hide their true feelings and lack precision or decisiveness.

Top tips for success

1. Try drawing your tree first at home. It may tell you a lot about yourself.

2. Position each tree in the centre of the page. Each one should, ideally, take up three-quarters of the page.

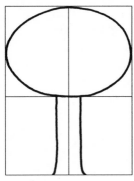

3. Do not draw in the roots. Your tree should be standing square on the ground.

4. Draw the trunk and the branches clearly and firmly in unbroken, parallel (not wavy) lines.

5. Do not draw lumps or nicks or isolated branches low down on the trunk.

6. Spread your branches equally on both sides of the crown of the tree.

7. Do not draw in leaves, flowers or fruit.

8. Do not draw animals in the tree (birds, monkeys, etc.), or features on the landscape (telephone box, litter bin, etc.) or any surrounding countryside.

Now draw your own tree

PROJECTIVE TESTS (5) – THE ARTHUS VILLAGE TEST

The Village Test originated at the Utrecht Institute of Professional Orientation and has been adapted for use in many European countries, notably in France by Henri Arthus. It has two parts: the first is non-verbal, and involves the construction of a village; the second is a questionnaire.

MATERIALS FOR THE TEST

In the version most widely used today, the materials consists of a small square table and 125 elements divided into four categories:

- 18 buildings with signs: sheep pen, butcher, office, café, dance hall, forge, train station, police station, hotel, launderette, town hall, fashion shop, gift shop, mill, chemist, post office, clothes shop and shoe shop

- 34 architectural elements: five bridges and 29 building blocks including the main part of 12 houses, 15 roofs and a church (main body and tower)

- 40 landscape elements: 34 trees, two animals, four human figures

- 33 unstructured elements: barriers, walls and posts to mark pathways and properties, a river

Candidates must use the elements provided to build a village.

The questionnaire used today has 30 questions which may vary according to the way in which the interview is ordered.

DURATION

Not precise. It usually takes between 15 and 35 minutes to do the building work and 15 to 45 minutes for the questionnaire.

QUESTIONNAIRE FOR THE VILLAGE TEST

- Are you right- or left-handed?

- Did you invent your village?

- Which direction does it face?

- What is the surrounding countryside like?

- Is there a river? Is there a forest?

- How does one gain access to your village?

- How does one get around your village?

- How does one get out of your village?

- What important buildings are there?

- Is there a castle, a factory or a prison in your village? Where are they?

- If you could choose to live in one house in this village, which one would it be?

- How old are you and what is your profession in this village?

- If your mother, your father or some members of your family were to live in this village, where would they live? Where would you live?

- Who are the village authorities?

- Who are the most important people in the village?

- The village is about to be attacked. By whom? How? Where?

- Does the village defend itself? If so, how?

- Once the attack is over, what state is the village in?

- You take a walk in the village. Where do you go?

- There is a fire in the village. Where is it? How did it start? What happens?

- What state is the village in after the fire?

- Someone is coming to visit the village. Who is the visitor? What are they going to do?

- If you could choose the inhabitants of your village, who would you choose?

- There is an unhappy child in this village. Where do they live? Why are they unhappy?

- Were there any pieces missing from your village? If so, which ones?

- Were there any pieces which bothered you? If so, which ones?

- Did you have a plan when you started? Did you change your plan as you were building?

- What would you change in this village? Where?

- Are you satisfied with your village?

- If I told you that you had to do something with the materials you have not used, what would you do with them?

ASSESSMENT OF RESULTS

The results are assessed according to several criteria:

- Materials used

  Number and percentage of pieces used for the village as a whole and for the four different categories

- Use of space

  Number and percentage of zones and sub zones (10-cm squares) occupied

- Organisation of the village

  Positioning in relation to four main zones (upper left, upper right, lower left, lower left), openings and pathways through village

- Positioning of symbolic elements: the builder's house, the church, bridges, trees (round and conical), arch

- General attitude and behaviour during the test (reaction times, order of movements, remarks, facial expressions, etc.)

INTERPRETATION OF RESULTS

The results are interpreted according to various data supplied by the spatial symbolism, the type of structure and the individual's body image.

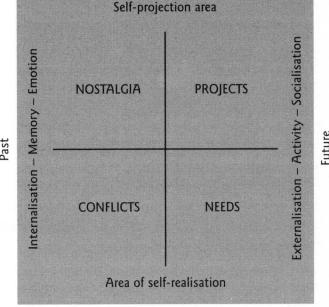

Spatial symbolism

The same spatial symbolism is used as in the Tree Test (see page 117). The village is divided into four zones and interpreted according to the schema below. The interpretation depends on the proportion of elements in each zone and how they are divided up.

For example, a majority of elements in the 'nostalgia' zone suggest an introverted personality who lives in the past; if the builder's house is placed in the 'conflict' zone, this suggests emotional problems.

Typical structures

The village may also be interpreted in terms of its structure. There are five main types of structure:

- Concentric, where the centre represents the subject

- Transverse limitations (roads or rivers crossing the village from left to right)

- Vertical communication (roads or rivers crossing the village from top to bottom)

- Cruciform (combination of the two previous types)

- Pivotal, where the village may be any shape, centred on a focal point

Body image

The way we perceive space may depend on the way we perceive our bodies, so the interpretation becomes that of the individual's body image. There are certain constants in this method of interpretation:

- The organisation of the village around a centre: translates as a reasonably strong and accepted personality

- Shield formation (arcs around a central point): egocentric personality

- Centre towards the top: inferiority complex

- Central statue: exhibitionist tendencies, problems in relating to others

- No centre: conformity and feelings of guilt

- Symmetrical construction: anxiety and insecurity

- Circular construction: internalisation of emotions, schizoid tendencies

- Square or angular construction: defence mechanism against insecurity and aggressive tendencies

- Semi-circle without a centre: phobic tendencies

- Ring structure with nothing in the centre: tendency to exaggerate or tell lies

- Horseshoe shape: paranoid tendencies

Top tips for success

1. Use as many elements as possible (average percentage of total for adults: 85 per cent).

2. Use an equal number of elements from each of the four categories.

3. Use up as much space as possible without scattering the pieces unduly.

4. Spread your buildings in more or less equal proportions throughout the four major areas.

5. Organise your village around a central area.

6. Position all the named buildings and the church.

7. Avoid symmetry.

8. Use curves (denoting emotions) and straight lines (logic) in equal proportions.

9. Do not forget to provide for openings and paths of communication.

10. Read the questionnaire and give it some thought.

COLOUR TESTS – PFISTER'S PYRAMID TEST

Some projective tests use the symbolism of colours. Of these, the Pyramid Test, designed in 1946 by Pfister, a Swiss psychologist, and later improved by Heiss and Hiltmann, two German psychologists, is the colour test most widely used today.

AIM

To evaluate the emotional response of a subject at a specific time: impulsiveness, feelings, maturity, empathy, etc.

FORMAT

For the test you are provided with:

- A piece of paper on which a five-storey pyramid is drawn using 15 2.5-cm squares

- Coloured squares of glossy paper in two or three different shades of ten colours in total (red, orange, yellow, blue, green, purple, brown, white, grey and black) with 45 pieces in each shade

The squares are spread out in front of you. You have to use them to cover the 15 squares of the pyramid.

You may be asked to make a row of three pyramids, each as aesthetically pleasing as possible; or you may have to make up three very ugly ones.

EVALUATION

For each pyramid, both the colours used and their layout are important factors in the evaluation process. The layout of the colours within the pyramid is a reflection of the way your personality is organised. Your choice of colours is, however, symptomatic of your emotional state.

The layout of the colours
The essential difference is between those who see and organise the pyramid as a flat surface and those who see it and organise it as a volume.

There are three main ways of building the structure: flat, stratified and structured.

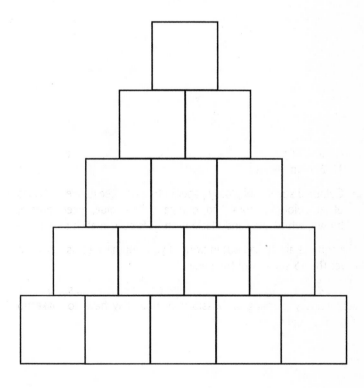

The flat pyramid
Statistically only a small minority (19 per cent) of people tested make this type of pyramid. A disordered layout is a sign of a inconsistency or weakness in the ego. Violent contrasts between the colours express feelings of anxiety. The use of a single colour and designs interspersed with white squares are signs of detachment from reality.

The stratified pyramid
Several colours used in successive layers: 29 per cent of people tested build this type of pyramid. Although indicating emotional maturity, this approach is nevertheless very laboured and methodical.

The structured pyramid
This type of pyramid occurs when the colours are chosen and laid out according to a well-thought-out plan. A total of 52 per cent of candidates build this type of pyramid.

Symmetry of colour or shape is interpreted as symptomatic of internalisation, with varying degrees of neurosis. On the other hand, deliberate asymmetry is a sign of an easily influenced, impressionable ego. Stepped architecture is also highly suggestive; in two colours, it indicates internal conflicts and when multi-coloured, it suggests feelings of insecurity.

Colour symbolism
Colours have particular emotional nuances. This is nothing new. The pyramid test has provided statistical proof. The interpretations are as follows:

Red: Feelings are strongly instinctive. Intense, hasty, short-lived emotions. Spontaneous and easily influenced; a tendency to impulsiveness, anger and occasional childish behaviour.

Orange: Feelings dominate instinct. Behaviour is stable despite the occasional tendency to overestimate one's abilities or to experience feelings of persecution.

Yellow: Calculating, lucid and driven. Clear-cut likes and dislikes. High levels of motivation and ambition, but always under control in terms of direction and use of time. Displays initiative but has low tolerance.

Green: Sensitivity and sociability dominate. Intuitive, makes friends easily, good communicator.

Pale green: Extrovert.

Dark green: Introvert with occasional emotional problems.

Blue: Dominated by reason, emotions are under control.

Dark blue: A tendency to over-rationalise. A rigid mind-set is indicated if all other colours are eschewed.

Purple: Sensitivity and creativity of prime importance. Emotional difficulties and instability when purple is the dominant colour.

Brown: Integrity, moral rectitude, consistent behaviour patterns. On the downside: obstinacy, rigidity, intolerance to change.

White: Rarely used. The over-use of white is a sign of detachment from reality. Systematically associated with red, it suggests aggressive impulses, explosive reactions.

Grey: Also little used. If used in small quantities it suggests prudence, discretion and a degree of mistrust. Over-use is a sign of neurotic tendencies.

Black: Characterised by neuroses and problems associated with puberty. Used to excess, it suggests depressive or suicidal tendencies.

Top tips for success

1. Build only structured pyramids.

2. Avoid being too symmetrical or asymmetrical in the way you arrange colours.

3. Use several colours in each line.

4. Do not use white, grey or black squares, with the possible exception of one or two for artistic effect.

5. Use all the different shades of any one colour.

6. Avoid exaggerated contrasts or opposites in your choice of colours.

7. Mix cold (blue, green, purple, etc.) and warm (red, orange, yellow, etc.) colours in the same proportions.

ROLE PLAY

Role play, sometimes called a situation exercise, or assessment centre, relies for its validity on the principle 'If you've done it once, you can do it again'. If a candidate is capable of resolving a problem in a simulated situation, it is reasonable to suppose that he or she will be also be able to do so when faced with real problems.

The US Army has been using this method successfully for a long time, and increasingly now it is being used by companies, particularly for recruiting young graduates who cannot be judged on their previous professional experience. Most experts agree that this is one of the most reliable of all selection methods, and in fact it may be the most reliable of all.

FORMAT

There are four steps to the selection procedure.

Firstly, there is the **individual interview,** during which you are asked to describe a successful activity for which you were responsible.

Secondly, there will be a **group discussion.** You are grouped with seven or eight other candidates and given a precise role within a scenario that simulates a professional situation. For example, you may be asked to imagine you are working in a travel agency where you have to promote the attractions of the geographical area which has been assigned to you; alternatively, you may be in a business meeting where no one is in agreement, but you must find common ground. In each simulation, the aim is not so much to split the candidates into winners and losers as to assess the way in which each participant relates to the others. Is he a leader or a troublemaker? Is she a follower or a mediator? And so on. Don't turn it into a competition. You run the risk of being ruled out if you insist on fighting your corner.

Thirdly, you will be given an **enigma** (for example: 'Who killed Dennis Ryan?'), which you have to solve in 20 minutes by asking questions of the interviewer. After 20 minutes, you have five minutes to make up your mind and give your answer. You are judged on the way you work (relevance of the questions asked, quality of the analysis, logic, etc.) and the speed with which you make decisions.

Finally, you will be taken on a **guided tour**, a factory visit after which you have to give your impressions orally in front of an invited audience. That is when you are assessed according to the sense and the pertinence of your observations

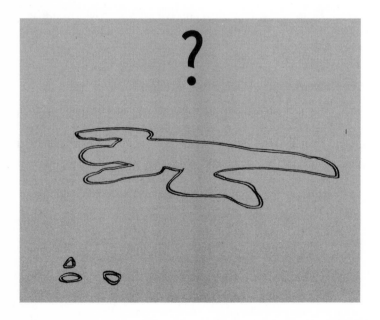

GRAPHOLOGY

There has been a significant increase in the use of graphology in relation to staff recruitment in the last 15 years or so. Handwriting is an unconscious response to the signals of the brain, a silent gesture that marks the identity and personality of the writer, almost without their knowing it. Many companies now use handwriting samples as part of their selection procedure although they may not acknowledge this publicly. However, if you are asked to submit an application form completed in your own handwriting, or accompanied by a handwritten letter, you may be fairly sure this is what it is intended for.

AIMS

Graphology can be employed to determine what a candidate ought to do and which career or job he or she appears most suited to pursue. It is an excellent tool for helping an employer to make a final selection from a short list of candidates. It indicates the individual's attitude to social relationships, reveals their level of education and measures their values and abilities according to age and experience. It will show the true ability of the writer, as opposed to their stated ambitions.

Graphologists are employed in one of two ways: they may either be told for which job the candidate is applying, so that they may look specifically for qualities best suited to the post, or they may work 'blind', simply reporting on what is detected from a submitted sample and leaving the employers to make up their own minds.

FORMAT

You may be asked to submit a sample of your handwriting. However, a more usual practice is to ask candidates to accompany any application form, CV, etc., with a handwritten covering letter. Alternatively, they may be asked to complete the application form in their own handwriting. This sample will then be analysed.

INTERPRETATION

A graphologist will be able to pick out the following salient points of character:

Working qualities: Leadership, personal discipline, organisational ability, capacity to work with others at all levels, accuracy and tenacity of purpose.

Temperament: Self-reliance, nervousness, excitability and serenity.

Intellectual qualities: Mental perception, logic and reasoning powers, memory and judgement, level of intelligence and education.

Social tendencies: Introversion or extroversion, levels of imagination, humour, inhibition, egotism and self-assertion.

Having thus established the particular characteristics of the candidate's personality, the graphologist will be able to make recommendations as to the suitability of the candidate for types of work or particular roles within a company.

CHARACTERISTICS OF HANDWRITING AND THEIR MEANINGS

It must be said, first and foremost, that there is no point in trying to disguise your handwriting in order to make what you regard as a favourable impression on your prospective employer. However, knowledge of some basic elements of graphology may help you to assess your own suitability for types of work.

Forward slant
The more handwriting slants to the right, the more emotionally responsive the writer. A particularly pronounced slant may indicate that it may take some time to get the writer back on an even keel after any disturbance.

Writers showing this characteristic are best suited to ever-changing conditions; they thrive on the stimulus of change and anything new. They like people and get on well with them, and are at their best when they have to sell themselves all the time. They are amongst the most natural salespeople in the world, but selling for a living is, surprisingly, not their forte, for they do not take well to anything that requires detailed record-keeping.

They do, however, respond readily to atmosphere, both positively and negatively. When depressed, they do not stay down for long. They have an in-built, natural resilience and bounce back quickly after set-backs. These writers are well placed in jobs where they have to deal with other people.

Upright script
Vertical handwriting (give or take a few degrees) shows an individual with a far more objective view of life. These writers rarely act on impulse; they are more inclined to stand back first and assess the problem, then ask themselves if the action they are considering will have the desired result for all concerned. They are forthright, but rarely speak without first considering all their options. Others may feel they are cold-blooded because of this. It is rare for these individuals to lose control in public.

When it comes to business decisions, partnerships can suffer, for these writers will not take into account the human factor. They make their decisions based only on the facts and figures to hand. Feelings do not come into it.

Reclined handwriting
Writing that slopes backwards denotes individuals who do not trust others easily. By writing in such a fashion, they are pulling away from people, life and even their obligations in some cases. These writers fear failure and making mistakes, a fear often rooted in an event or series of incidents in their past.

They make good 'back-room boys', workers in the background who keep things running. Not much fazes them because little is allowed to upset their carefully held composure. (Note, however, that left-handed writers frequently have a natural backward slant which does not indicate any of the above.)

Size
Small handwriting suggests an ability to concentrate for long periods at a time, where large writing means quite the opposite.

Other features of style and content
Little loops in the stem of the letters 'd' and 't' imply sensitivity to criticism but also a person who thrives on any form of personal appreciation, which will always ensure their loyalty.

Left-handedness implies quicker than average perceptiveness.

Over-use of the word 'I' in a letter will suggest that the writer has a great sense of their self-importance. A letter which avoids using 'I' altogether indicates that the writer takes very objective, dispassionate view of events.

Underlining of words indicates uncertainty or diffidence.

Your signature will tell a great deal about you – placed in the centre it indicates confidence, but too far to the right and you will be considered overly so. A signature at the left-hand side of a letter indicates someone who needs to be different.

Top tips for submitting a handwriting sample

1. Follow **exactly** any instructions you are given: for example, if you are asked to print, or use capitals, do not write in your usual handwriting – and vice versa.

2. Write on white – or cream, or another neutral-coloured – paper. Do not use brightly coloured paper.

3. Use plain, not lined paper. If you need a guide to keep lines straight, place one under the sheet of paper you are writing on.

4. Write with a pen, never a pencil or fibre-tip, and preferably use dark blue ink. Black ink is considered to indicate someone who needs to be understood immediately. Light blue indicates weakness of character. Coloured inks, such as brown, red and particularly green, are to be avoided. They indicate emotional immaturity. Fountain pens are acceptable, but may indicate a very precise nature (this may, of course, be to your advantage). Fibre tips suggest an emotionally-orientated character. Biros are probably the best option, indicating directness and immediacy.

5. Pay attention to presentation; write clearly, using even margins and line-spacing. Try not to let your handwriting deteriorate towards the end of the letter.

6. Lay out the letter in the way that you would any business letter. Start with your address, followed by the date (use 23 June 2000, not Monday 23rd, etc.) and the address of the person you are writing to, **exactly** as laid out on any letter you have received from the company. Do not use colloquialisms or old-fashioned style such as indented lines in an address.

7. Sign the letter with your usual signature, but try not to let it be larger than the name of the person you are writing to. Write your name clearly under the signature, but do not follow this with Ms/Miss/Mrs/Mr. Your marital status or title is irrelevant.

8. Remember that your mood at the time of writing will be evident. Do not write if you are feeling tired or angry, and if you write a letter in the evening, always check it carefully the following morning. The cold light of day tends to turn up any mistakes you had overlooked.

INTERVIEWS

Interviews are used by 99 per cent of companies and recruitment agencies. It is therefore essential that you develop good techniques for being interviewed, in order to put yourself in the best possible light for any post.

There are many different sorts of interview, including preliminary telephone interviews (to make an initial selection), face-to-face interviews with the person or persons responsible for recruitment and group interviews (primarily used for recruiting sales representatives). At this stage, providing the pre-selection has been done properly, there are only four or five candidates on the list, all with similar CVs in terms of qualifications, and all with the sort of profiles the company is seeking. The interview process enables a short list to be drawn up, ideally of just two candidates who will be presented to the company's top management.

INTERVIEW PREPARATION

An interview is not a spontaneous occasion. It requires careful forethought and preparation in terms of both content (what you are going to talk about) and appearance (the image of yourself that you wish to project).

Know the company
It is essential that you acquaint yourself as closely as possible with the company and the particular post for which you are applying. Thorough background knowledge will improve your interview performance by demonstrating your interest and will also give you confidence in answering questions. Find out as much as you can about the firm – its size, location, products, profitability, customers, etc. It is highly likely that you will be sent literature with all this information when you first enquire about a job. If you do not, a telephone call or a visit to the human resources department, if there is one, will furnish you with everything you need.

This is the time to gather as much information as you can about the job you are applying for – salary, holiday entitlement, pension plans, etc. Do not wait until the interview to ask such questions: any sign that you have not done your research beforehand will count against you.

Appearance

As far as appearance is concerned, the trend nowadays is towards conformity. Companies are increasingly likely to impose codes for dress (clothes or hairstyles which are too showy or eccentric are not appreciated) and even for behaviour – smoking, for example, is often discouraged and may be allowed only in certain designated areas. It is important to appear conventional and understated, all the more so if you are seeking an administrative post. However, if the position is creative or commercially orientated, it is acceptable to be more fashionable.

For men, the safest thing to wear is always a suit. For women, there are more options, which only make the question more difficult. However, the same general rules apply: opt for something fairly formal and conservative, a suit if possible, and avoid trousers unless you feel very strongly about them. Both sexes should keep jewellery to a minimum. Overall, aim for a clean, well-groomed appearance; you wish to appear efficient, well disciplined and in control.

YOUR PERFORMANCE AT THE INTERVIEW

It is important that you create the right impression from the very start of the interview. Remember to knock before you enter the room and walk in with as much confidence as you can muster. Don't forget to smile when you greet the interviewer. Wait for the interviewer to extend a hand before you try to shake hands and sit down when invited to do so.

Your handshake

Your handshake reveals a great deal about you. If it is too brief or your grip is floppy, it reflects either a lack of consideration for the other person or weakness and lack of purpose. If it is over-enthusiastic, it indicates a tendency to bluff and even an element of obsequiousness. A short, firm handshake is best.

Body language

From the moment you walk into the room, a good interviewer is observing your mannerisms and drawing his or her own conclusions. Ideally, you want to give the impression that you feel good and at ease without appearing too casual; try to be both relaxed and attentive. Never lose sight of the fact that your body language and your facial expressions say it all. Avoid the following:

• Slouching and putting your hands in your pockets

• Leaning too close to the interviewer

• Gesticulating

Certain gestures may contradict your words or reveal you as a sham. Many recruitment consultants have a basic training in the technique of interpreting your body language. You can't pretend that you are a willing candidate if you slide down in your chair and look out of the window. Nor, apparently, will you appear dynamic if your left hand is resting on the right (the opposite if you are left-handed). You will also be considered insincere if you keep covering your mouth with your hands. Try not to cross and uncross your legs repeatedly (this can indicate impatience or even sexual problems), and don't fidget (this is taken as a sign of nervousness or instability).

Answering the questions

Remember that the aim of the interview is to give appropriate information about you to your prospective employer. To this end, try to keep your answers pertinent and short. If you are asked to talk about yourself, do not give your interviewer a life story and do not be tempted to blow your own trumpet too much: by all means, show that you are ambitious but also that you are willing to wait and to learn. Restrict your replies to an account of your relevant experience and expertise, and the skills and qualities you consider you will bring to the job.

Top tips for giving the right impression

1. Dress smartly

2. Shake hands firmly but quickly

3. Sit upright and look as though you are paying attention – do not avoid the interviewer's eyes

4. Try to appear relaxed

5. Speak clearly and know when to stop

6. Make a dignified exit

Keep your answers informative and brief. Usually interviewers avoid personal questions, but if they do stray (to test your reactions) then deal with it subtly. Pinpoint and elaborate on certain points in your CV that you think are particularly important.

Avoid answering 'Yes' and 'No' to questions; expand your responses so you give a full picture of what you think. Don't talk about what the company can do for you (that's not important to them) but do make clear what you feel you can do for them.

Avoid jokes, sarcasm, irony and any purely anecdotal remarks.

THE CONTENT OF THE INTERVIEW

It is important that you prepare your answers to likely questions. Practise out loud beforehand, if you can, and devise answers to typical questions. Do plenty of 'homework' if you are applying for a job that requires special technical expertise.

You are likely to be asked about your home background, your studies at school or college and what your past jobs have been. Prepare full, honest answers, emphasising any positive aspects, such as people who have encouraged you, relevant interests and skills. Make sure you will never be tempted to reply 'I don't know'.

Do not ramble, and avoid talking about unhappy episodes in your life and career, disputes with previous employers, etc.

Typical questions

Some questions arise at almost every interview and you should have replies prepared for them. You are almost certain to be asked about:

- Your interests outside work (make sure you have some)

- Your previous employer

- Why you want this job

- Your ambitions

- Your qualifications, skills, familiarity with particular machines, equipment, etc.

- Your health, and that of your family

Other commonly asked questions include:

'Why do you want to work with our company?'

As ever, honesty is the name of the game, so do not try to use flattery to weasel your way in. This is the opportunity for you to show that you have researched the company and the job, and to demonstrate your enthusiasm for both. Do not under any circumstances say that you don't have a particular reason.

'What do you think are your particular strengths/weaknesses'

To be credible, you must stick to the truth, but remember that you should also be positive. There is no point in mentioning that you are not a morning person or that your second language is a bit rusty, but don't paint yourself as a complete saint either; no one is perfect and you won't fool anyone. Play it straight but don't give them any information that could allow them to undermine your position.

Be clear about your positive qualities without going overboard. Concentrate on the things you can bring to the job. Never be drawn into a discussion of your weaknesses – you must acknowledge that you have shortcomings, but simply say that you do not think you have any that will affect your suitability for the job.

'Would you be happy to move to work elsewhere with the company/work at weekends?'

Don't take this type of question too literally. Make it clear that you are willing to make sacrifices, within reason – but that you may expect something in return.

'Do you consider yourself to be self-motivated in your work?'

Yes, of course you are, but don't forget to mention that you are also a good (and enthusiastic) team player. Beware of this type of leading question and try to avoid giving a one-sided view of yourself.

Awkward questions

You may be asked a question that you find almost impossible to answer. Some interviewers delight in wrong-footing candidates, in order to test their reactions under stress. If this happens, try to remain calm; ask for explanation of the question if necessary – this will give you time to think and will certainly avoid you giving a muddled reply to something you don't understand.

You may be asked to sell yourself. Prepare your reply to this one beforehand – aim to emphasise your good qualities but don't oversell yourself or sound as though you are boasting.

If you are asked something you don't know, but should – details of the job you are applying for which were given in the original advertisement, for example – don't try to bluff your way out. Remain calm and admit your mistake. But, better still, make sure you look over all the details you have before you go into the interview, so that this doesn't happen.

Before you answer

Before you reply to any question, ask yourself:

- What is the interviewer really trying to find out?

- How can I use this to show myself in a positive light?

- What should I definitely NOT say about this?

QUESTIONS FOR YOU TO ASK

If you are asked if you have any questions, use this as another opportunity to demonstrate your interest. Remember, however, not to ask questions about pay, working conditions etc., which you should have researched beforehand. Questions about further details of the job, any monitoring/assessment procedures within the company, further training opportunities and future responsibilities will all be well received. If you have no questions, simply explain that everything has been made clear during the interview.

ENDING AN INTERVIEW

Once again, preparation and mental rehearsal are the keys to good technique. Remember to say goodbye, shaking hands once more and make a smooth exit from the room. Do not forget to collect any belongings, such as your handbag or umbrella, you may have had with you.

PREPARING AN EFFECTIVE CURRICULUM VITAE

Although this book focuses on test and interview procedures, you will not even reach that stage if your initial contact with the company concerned does not impress on them that you are someone they should look at more closely. Preparing an effective CV is therefore a vital part of the process of finding and securing that all-important job.

As with all the other aspects of finding employment that have been dealt with in this book, the keys are preparation and focus. Spend time working on a good CV and your efforts will be repaid. Throw together a list of your qualifications and previous employment in an unattractive document and you will be wasting your time in practising techniques for doing well in selection tests because you will not get a chance to exercise them.

THE PURPOSE OF THE CV

If the job you want is worth having, the chances are that plenty of other people will want it as well. The human resources manager, or whoever is dealing with the applications, will receive a large number of written applications. They will have to read all those applications and use them to make a selection of which candidates to invite for interview. Whether or not you are offered an interview depends on how you present yourself in your CV and whether it communicates your skills and enthusiasm to the employer sufficiently well to impress them. A good CV is your entry-point to an interview. If you fall at this hurdle, you have lost the job and you are back to square one. You can't get more important than that.

It is therefore worth spending a little time thinking about what you need to include on your CV, and how it is going to be used, before you set finger to keyboard. Start by putting yourself in the position of that human resources manager and think carefully about their requirements. If you do that, some of the important factors in preparing your CV become straightforward common sense.

Your CV is your first contact with the company. In the same way that a well-groomed applicant will make a good initial impression, a well-presented document, clearly laid out, concise and to the point, will have a good impact and is more likely to be read with attention.

A CV should give a comprehensive but workable snapshot of your education, qualifications, experience and skills. If it is too long, it will be off-putting. If it is too short, you may miss out vital factors. Keep it concise and targeted.

The company knows the sort of person they are looking for and the skills that person should display. Match the focus of your CV with the qualities they are asking for and that you can deduce will be essential for the job. Do your homework.

While you are aiming to show yourself in the best possible light, you must be honest. Don't be tempted to make misleading or ambiguous statements that will lead the employer to the wrong conclusions.

CONTENT

As the name suggests, your CV should include details of everything about you that is relevant to your employment. Every CV is unique, so there may be areas listed here that you will not need to include, but in general, the content of your CV will fall under the following headings.

Biographical details
This section gives the employer all the essential details about you. You should include the following information:

• Name, making clear which is your surname.

• Title.

- Address.

- Telephone number, with a work or mobile contact if appropriate.

- E-mail address.

- Date of birth and age.

- Nationality.

- Marital status and children.

It may be appropriate to include other specific information here, such as whether you hold a clean driving licence and that you are in a good state of health.

Education history
Here you need to say where you have been educated. List your senior schools and colleges with their addresses and the dates you attended. The most recent dates should be at the top of the list. For example:

2000–2003 University of Reading
           Whiteknights, Reading, RG6 4XY

1993–2000 Loughton County High School
           Roding Lane, Loughton, Essex, CM57 4HU

Qualifications
List the examinations you have taken, the date of the examinations and the grades you achieved, with the highest grades listed first. Specify if you are awaiting results. Again, the most recent qualifications should be at the top. For example:

2003 **BA (Hons)**
      History   (Results awaited)

2000 **GCSE A Levels**
      History   A
      Physical Education   B
      Biology   B

1999 **GCSE AS Level**
      Business Studies   B

1998	**GCSEs**	
	History	A
	Biology	A
	Resistant materials	A
	Physical education	B
	English language	B
	English literature	B
	Mathematics	B
	Physics	B
	French	C
	Chemistry	C

Non-academic achievements

This section gives you a chance to show a broader involvement in extra-curricular activities, sports or other organisations. Include such things as Duke of Edinburgh awards, sporting achievements, etc. This and the next two sections should show where your natural talents lie and how you have made the most of them.

Responsibilities

Extending the previous section, or perhaps as part of that section, focus here on areas in which you have taken special responsibility, such as head girl, boy or prefect at school, chairperson or committee member of a club, captain of a sports team, director of a school play.

Leisure interests

The employer is trying to find out what sort of person you are, and this will help them to do that. Only include areas that really interest you, group them into related themes and try to show a balance of activities if possible.

Previous employment record

Your employment record should be listed with the most recent employment at the top. List the dates, the company name and location, the job title and a brief description of your role in the company.

For senior positions, it may be appropriate to give more information on your responsibilities, especially for the most recent job. More specific dates may be useful in some cases. You are looking to communicate the key skills and responsibilities of each post.

If you are applying for your first full-time job, list your vacation employment and work experience.

1998–2000	**PLI Advertising**	**Junior account executive**
		General office organisation, liaison with clients, writing advertising copy; reporting directly to the account executive
1996–1998	**Smith's Shoes**	**Sales assistant**
		Saturday and holiday employment serving customers, restocking displays, maintaining stock lists

Career objectives
This should be a very concise statement of your primary skills and the direction in which you would like your career to move. For example:

I am a practical and resourceful person with strong interpersonal skills who enjoys contributing to a team but responds well to responsibility. I have a flexible outlook at this early stage of my career, but I feel that would be most suited to a career in human resources.

Referees
Give two referees, choosing people in responsible positions so that their references have authority, but making sure that you have actually worked with them so that they can be specific in their comments. There is no point giving the managing director of a company if you have only ever seen him in the foyer of the office building. The people chosen are most usually your manager at your current job, your tutor or head of department at college or university, or your head teacher or head of year at school.

Always check with the person that they are happy to act as a referee and let them know each time you send your CV to a prospective employer.

PRESENTATION

Everyone has access to a computer and there is no excuse for a poorly presented CV. Use good-quality, plain white A4 paper, printed in black on one side only using a clear and classic font such as Times. Space out the text so that it is attractive and easy to read, and use bold or italic sparingly to highlight headings or important elements. Check where the page breaks fall so that the text is logically grouped and you do not have a heading at the bottom of a page, for example, separated from its following text.

Always check every aspect of the CV carefully, both on screen and on a printed draft. If possible, ask someone else to check it through. It is very easy to miss a typing mistake, for example, when you have spent a long time working on the document. Spelling or grammatical mistakes make a poor impression, as does trying to use complex words or sentences when a simple one will do. Remember the marketing mnemonic KISS: Keep It Simple, Stupid!

UPDATING AND AMENDING

Keep the CV on disk so that you can easily update and amend it as necessary. Add new information – such as exam results – as they become available and make amendments if you find that an employer has misunderstood one section or required more detail in another.

Before you send out your CV, go through it carefully in relation to the specific job for which you are applying and make appropriate changes. For example, you may want to highlight particular aspects of one of your previous jobs to show specific skills, or develop your list of leisure interests.

ACCOMPANYING DOCUMENTS

You may be asked to supply copies of your degree or other certificates to accompany the CV. Send only what is requested but have any additional documentation readily available so that you can fulfil any subsequent requests quickly and efficiently.

You should also send an accompanying letter with your CV, and many companies prefer this to be handwritten so that they can assess whether you can produce a neat and legible letter. Set out the letter according to the standard custom and write clearly in black or blue ink on good-quality plain white or headed A4 paper. Keep the margin widths consistent at about 2.5 cm/1 in all round and write in straight lines across the page. Head the letter with the name of the vacancy and location of the advertisement, if appropriate.

The letter should be concise and to the point, stating in a few sentences why you are applying for the job and defining the major reasons why you feel you should be considered.

APPLICATION FORMS

Some firms may ask you to fill in an application form rather than sending your CV, but the work you have done in compiling your CV will be equally useful in this case. Always read through the whole application form first to make sure you fill in the correct information in the right places. You may like to take a photocopy of the document and write a rough copy first; that way, you can space out the information clearly and not run out of space when you are filling in all your qualifications! Write clearly, answer honestly, and think about what the employer needs to know about you in each instance.

REACHING THE TARGET

Use a large plain envelope for your CV; don't try to squeeze it into a small envelope. Address it clearly to the relevant person by name, with their job title, company and an accurate address. If you do not have all the details, telephone the office and ask. Always use first-class post.

Confidence in your own ability is the key to getting that job. Look at your skills objectively, take pride in your achievements and work on your weaknesses – and you will succeed.

INDEX

Strengthen your Performance in Psychological Tests

Cecile Cesari

THE book for job candidates, with all the inside information on how selection tests work, the fundamental elements in the selection process and how to handle them to obtain the best results. Containing a good number of exercise examples to improve your understanding and build your confidence, plus explanation of outside, personal factors that may affect your performance. Learn to identify these factors and manage them effectively to present yourself in the best possible light.

ISBN: 0-572-02208-5

Train your Brain for a Fast-track Career

Dr Jacqueline Renaud

To illustrate your latent brain power potential, the author of this book likens it to that of a racehorse pulling a milk cart! The capacity of your brain power will amaze even yourself if you harness it and train it in the same way as you would your body. Learn how your brain works and, through structured exercises, strengthen your mental ability until you out-pace colleagues and managers alike. Take yourself to a higher level of achievement in every area of decision making.

ISBN: 0-572-02290-5

Strengthen your Memory

Michael Fidlow

Do you already know that your memory is suspect? If you do, this book can change that. You have two kinds of memory: natural and artificial and you can improve both by committing yourself to this book and learning how to re-organise your thinking. By employing these classic memory methods used the world over, you will be able to remember numbers, people, jokes and all the information you gain from everyday reading. In short, you can change your life.

ISBN: 0-572-01609-3

Gain the Power of Positive Thought

Gilbert Oakley

Life is all in the mind! If you think positively, then you will be successful; think negatively and everything seems to go wrong. Through a series of easy questionnaires, you can discover your personal areas of negative thinking, learn to focus on them and, ultimately, destroy them. Once you have passed that hurdle, follow an eight-day, step-by-step positive development course that could change your life. Don't miss this opportunity.

ISBN: 0-572-02336-7